From
Laurel Hill
to Siler's Bog

FROM LAUREL HILL TO SILER'S BOG

❧ The Walking Adventures of a Naturalist

BY JOHN K. TERRES

with illustrations by Charles L. Ripper
and a new introduction by
C. Ritchie Bell

ALGONQUIN BOOKS OF CHAPEL HILL

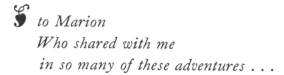 *to Marion*
Who shared with me
in so many of these adventures . . .

ALGONQUIN BOOKS OF CHAPEL HILL
Post Office Box 2225
Chapel Hill, North Carolina 27515–2225
ISBN 0–912697–26–1

"Search for The Golden Mouse" and "Trail of the
Little Gray Ghost" have previously appeared in
Audubon.

This book was originally published by
Alfred A. Knopf, Inc. Illustrations and typography
are those of the original edition, and are
reproduced by permission of Alfred A.
Knopf, Inc.

First Algonquin Books of Chapel Hill edition
Manufactured in the United States of America

It is the glory of God to conceal things,
but the glory of kings is to search things out.
Proverbs 25:2

Acknowledgments

e&   I am greatly indebted to the librarians of the Southern Historical Collections and the North Carolina Collections at the University of North Carolina for making available to me maps, papers, diaries, and books relating to the Morgan and Mason families and the Mason Farm, or Mason Plantation as it was once known; to Dr. Louis R. Wilson of the University Library for sending me his book *Selected Papers of Mrs. Cornelia Phillips Spencer.* Without these materials Chapter I, The Story of an Old Farm, could not have been written.

I am grateful to the University of North Carolina authorities for allowing me to roam at will over the Mason Farm for the last eight years and to Dr. C. Ritchie Bell of the Botany Department for making the botanical research area of the Mason Farm available to me for my wildlife studies. I offer my apologies to him for changing the name of his Botany Lake to Muskrat Pond.

I owe special thanks to Dr. H. W. Totten and to Dr. Albert E. Radford of the Botany Department for helping me to identify especially difficult groups of plants and to Dr. Charles E. Jenner and Dr. William L. Engels of the Zoology Department for many kindnesses and the resources of their department. Walter H. Wheeler, Professor of Geology at the University of North Carolina, was particularly helpful in explaining the geology of the region.

Duncan Cuyler of Durham gave me a course of instruction in identifying the dragonflies of Muskrat Pond, and Dr. Peter H. Klopfer, Animal Behaviorist and Associate Professor of Zoology, Duke University at Durham, assisted me greatly with his suggestions of how to observe animals at night.

I am particularly grateful to Dr. Phillips Russell, Professor Emeritus of Creative Writing, University of North Carolina, for his constant encouragement in the writing of this book and for critically reading parts of the manuscript. And my special thanks to Joe Jones, naturalist, local historian, and an alumnus of the University of North Carolina, who introduced me to the Mason Farm and accompanied me there on many of my trips.

JOHN K. TERRES
1969

Contents

Dam

Muskrat
Pond

Concr
Dam

Where Great
Horned Owl
Caught
Muskrat

Weed-grown
Field

The *Mason* *Farm*

Laurel

By *Charles L. Ripper*
from a sketch by
John K. Terres

Yancey

Hill

Brook

Den-Trees
of Flying
Squirrels

Hickory Tree
of Flying
Squirrels

Nest of
Great
Horned Owl

Woods

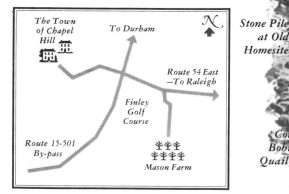

The Town
of Chapel
Hill

To Durham

N

Stone Pile
at Old
Homesite

Nest of
Golden
Mouse

Route 54 East
—To Raleigh

Finley
Golf
Course

Lone
Field

Barred Ou
Nest in Top
of Dead Tr

Route 15-501
By-pass

Mason Farm

Covey of
Bobwhite
Quail, and
Nest

Nest of
Bobwhite
Quail

Siler

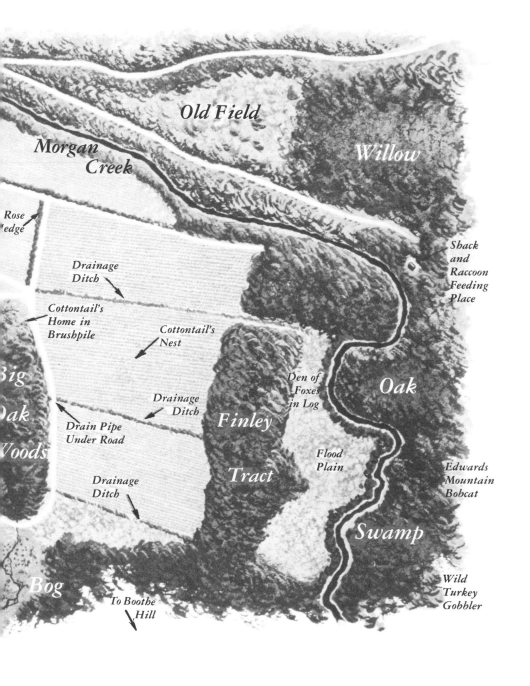

Old Field

Morgan Creek

Willow

Rose Hedge

Drainage Ditch

Cottontail's Home in Brushpile

Cottontail's Nest

Shack and Raccoon Feeding Place

Big Oak Woods

Drainage Ditch

Drain Pipe Under Road

Finley

Den of Foxes in Log

Oak

Drainage Ditch

Tract

Flood Plain

Edwards Mountain Bobcat

Swamp

Bog

To Boothe Hill

Wild Turkey Gobbler

Introduction

Here, on the last six hundred wild acres of the historic Mason Farm, where "the fields and woods are in balance and the numbers and varieties of wild things reach their richest and fullest expression," an incredible demonstration has been going on over the past twenty years since John Terres walked the land and wrote with singular accuracy, interest, and expression of its many inhabitants. The red-tailed hawks still soar and dive over the green fields; owls still call in the winter stillness of the Big Oak Woods; deer continue to browse the woodland margins; and the tracks of raccoon, fox, and bobcat still occur in the shallow snows of winter and along the muddy banks of Morgan Creek in summer.

But a rare thing has happened: the environmental clock has been turned back a bit. Today ospreys and even a bald eagle or two may be sighted "trying their luck" with the fishing at Muskrat Pond; the otters and fish that John Terres noted twenty years ago had been driven from Morgan Creek in the recent past by deadly sewage pollution are returning as the water quality of the stream is improved; and even beavers, absent in the area for many years, are once again building their dams and lodges in the shallow headwaters of our Piedmont streams. This land, now set aside as the Mason Farm Biological Research Reserve by the University of North Carolina at Chapel Hill, is a clear demonstration of the remarkable biological resiliency, or ecological regeneration, of a balanced natural area that is afforded a realistic degree of protection.

The Mason Farm lands, partly occupied and now administered by the North Carolina Botanical Garden, are more biologically diverse, more interesting, and more beautiful than they were twenty years ago. With the protection afforded by an enlightened university and a cooperative town council, they are also more secure as a viable natural area that serves as a critical teaching and research resource for both present and future generations as they probe the limits of man's role in the balance of nature.

The great biological diversity and the exceptionally interesting natural history of these lands can always be savored through these wonderfully descriptive stories by John Terres; but fortunately "the sweep of fields, the wide woodlands and open sky" of the old Mason Farm remain much as they were a century or more ago, and can still be enjoyed through the seasons by all those who cherish our natural heritage.

It is here that I pay tribute, along with all those who worked for the preservation of the Mason Farm, to John Terres's book which inspired and stimulated so many of us and will continue to do so in the years ahead.

C. RITCHIE BELL
Director, North Carolina Botanical Garden

Author's Note

In January 1961, I arrived in Chapel Hill, North Carolina, from my home in New York City to finish the writing of a half-million-word encyclopedia of North American birds. I had no thought of writing any other book at that time—the encyclopedia alone was a project that needed my every attention. I had given up my job as editor of *Audubon* magazine to work on the encyclopedia full-time and had gone to Chapel Hill at the urging of my friend W. L. McAtee, a retired government biologist, editor, and writer. He had moved there because of its "small town atmosphere" and excellent reference libraries at the University of North Carolina at Chapel Hill; at Duke University, twelve miles away; and at the library of North Carolina State University at Raleigh.

In a small rented cottage at the end of a tree-lined lane, within walking distance of the university, I wrote steadily every day and far into the night. Within a few years I had written 300,000 words and had the book well on the way to completion. But during that time I found the one-man writing of an encyclopedia of bird life a project I could not work upon all the time and remain keen in mind and fresh in spirit. Most of my life I had tried to spend some hours of each day, or week, in the fields and woodlands so necessary to my happiness.

Shortly after I arrived in Chapel Hill, Joe Jones, a naturalist and managing editor of the local newspaper, *The Chapel Hill Weekly,* took me one day to see "the Mason Farm." I knew nothing of the place except that it was owned by the University of North Carolina. I began to walk over its land, filling my journals with sketches and notes about its wildlife and of the Southern trees, shrubs, vines, and wildflowers that grew there and provided the animals of the farm with a home. I had kept a journal of my nature observations for twenty-seven years; it was a habit I hoped to continue all my life.

In the beginning, I had no thought of writing a book about the Mason Farm—its romantic and ecological story—but within four years after I had arrived in Chapel Hill, I had filled six journals with 200,000 words about the wildlife of this North Carolina land. And within another four years, in eight additional journals, another 250,000. Soon I found that, without slighting the encyclopedia, my journals were comparable with it in numbers of words.

Dr. Francis Harper, a noted field biologist who had also retired to Chapel Hill, had sometimes traveled with me on my trips to the Mason Farm. He knew of the detailed notes I had been keeping of my observations. One day he said, "Why don't you write a book about the place?" At the time I did not take his suggestion seriously, but the more I thought of it, the more the idea appealed to me. My publishers, even though anxious for me to complete my encyclopedia, were interested in my story of the old farm. They approved, and I went to work.

ॐ In the summer of 1968, when I had almost finished the writing of this book, I received a letter from Dr. Louis R. Wilson of the Wilson Library of the University of North Carolina at Chapel Hill. It was about a biographical sketch of me that had appeared simultaneously in several North Carolina newspapers, relating some of my experiences with the wildlife of the Mason Farm. In his letter, Dr. Wilson expressed great interest in my studies of the natural life of the place, and he wrote that he was sending me, for my reference, a complimentary copy of the *Selected Papers of Mrs. Cornelia Phillips Spencer,* a local author, whose most active writing career at Chapel Hill had been from 1865 to the 1880's.

It is, in part, to acknowledge my debt to Mrs. Spencer's history of the Morgan and Mason families, who originally owned the land of my search, that I have written this brief tribute to one of the most remarkable women in North Carolina's history.

Besides her nineteenth-century letters, which are a social record of her times, and her pioneering work for the higher education of women, no one made more impassioned appeals for the preservation of the magnificent woodlands immediately about Chapel Hill, which even then were in danger of exploitation. Any threat of the despoliation or sale of university lands, Mrs. Spencer assailed with letters of such anguished charm that, through her efforts, land was restored to the university and woodlands were saved.

Dr. Wilson, in his Introduction to the *Selected Papers,* wrote that he had chosen them "to show how one woman, left a widow with an infant daughter in 1861 amid the desolation and poverty of the Civil War and degradation of Reconstruction, faced the problems of those dark periods and spurred North Carolina to the support of causes that have profoundly affected every phase of the State's life."

The last extensive wild land, close to its campus, owned by the University of North Carolina, is the Mason Farm. It is a land that Mrs. Spencer and the Mason Family loved for its birds and wild-flowers, its woodlands and sparkling waters, which were so much a part of her life and of the people of the university town who walked its fields and groves. It is in the spirit of Mrs. Spencer's love of pure waters and trees and all wild things and their preservation, and their study by students, faculty, and others, that I have written this book. It is to tell of the strengthening of body and mind to be found in the fragrant fields and marshes; to describe senses made razor-sharp watching wild animals by day or by night, with the simple joys of discovery; to sing the spiritual renewal that awaits one in these small wildernesses so close to home; and to relate, in the story of one North Carolina farm, the healing solitude of the still-wild lands, and our unending need for them. . . .

If I became philosophic about the wild things I studied on the Mason Farm, it was because I had learned to understand them. Over and over, the creatures of fur and feathers had shown me that they enjoyed living quite as much as I, or perhaps even more. With senses far keener than mine, they lived only from moment to moment, high-keyed, sensitive beyond powers of any human kind. For them, the instant is played to its fullest to satisfy some insistent need: to glory in savage pursuit, to taste quick fear and wild flight, to know in the next moment blessed forgetfulness or the full belly and innocent sleep.

To become a part of their world, I used methods known to hunters and photographers of wildlife—the blind, or "hide"—and skills of the wildlife management men—the live-trap, the mark on the individual animal, and then its release so that it may be followed and studied and recognized again.

What the naturalist needs, then, is as much of his days and nights as he can spare, to crouch motionless and in silence, cramped in a hidden observation place—a thicket, a canvas blind, a platform in a tree—his endurance and his interest holding him there through bitter cold or intense heat, hovering along some trail much traveled by the wild things he has chosen to observe.

It is in these small, wild places, refuges kept wild by their isolation and the protection of the animals in them, that the naturalist finds the Last Frontier. And in this much-civilized land he is that unusual paradox: both a cultured and a primitive man. With love for the wildlife that he studies, and with songs and poems in his heart, he has returned, hundreds or even thousands of years, to his hunter-trapper ancestors to learn the language of sign—the trail in the dust, the lone feather, the traces of wild fur on the tree—that tells him what animal has passed there, what it fed upon, and where it has gone. But when he crushes the grass under his feet, it springs up again, and there is no blood in his tracks.

From Laurel Hill to Siler's Bog

CHAPTER I

Story of an Old Farm

Once they are gone, the trees and the grasslands,
the screaming waterfowl, the beavers and the antelope,
we can only remember them with longing. We are not
God. We cannot make America over again as it was
in the beginning, but we can come to what is left
of our heritage with a patriot's reverence.

—DONALD CULROSS PEATTIE

I first saw the Mason Farm of the University of North Carolina at Chapel Hill in February 1961. For one who had lived too long in a great city, that day was the beginning of my first year in the rural South. There I was to experience some of my finest adventures in the natural world—a world I understood so much better than that of the cities.

I had been a naturalist most of my life, and my paternal grandfather, born and reared in Charlotte, had been a naturalist before me. I felt like a native who had come home. Crossing Morgan Creek over a concrete dam, I walked under the winter sun on a road that led over a grass-grown levee, built to hold back the spring floods. I had no thought of what might lie beyond.

When I reached the top of the dike, I gasped. For two miles straightaway, and from east to west, windswept fields and woods lay under an enormous vault of blue. A thousand acres of swamps and fields and forests, to as far as I could see, were suddenly opened before me—a vast freedom of land and sky. The farm, only two miles southeast of Chapel Hill, a city of 30,000, was near, yet isolated, a land few people knew. As I penetrated its old roads, I felt its loneliness that I was to know by day through silences broken only by a hawk's screaming or the shouting of crows and by night through the moaning of owls and the barking of half-wild dogs and foxes. This was a wilderness of the land to match a wilderness of the heart.

During the next seven and one half years, I walked five thousand miles and spent ten thousand hours there, searching the hidden wild things of its acres. The place names of their homes still ring sweet in my ears—the tinkle of Yancey Brook, the wind in the green forest of Laurel Hill, the old fields of whispering weeds and grasses, the sighing of the pines that border Siler's Bog. In spring and in summer I walked the fragrant aisles of Big Oak Woods where the wildflowers grew in wet glades, and under autumn suns I knew the sad isolation of Lone Field. And in every season I followed the silver ribbon of Morgan Creek that murmured softly in summer but in spring roared, a tempest of waters, into the dark mystery of Willow Oak Swamp.

⁊ This Piedmont land of the Mason Farm has changed in the

time of man. There is far less of the forest now, and some of its waters are polluted, but it still has granite uplands with rhododendron-lined streams that cut canyons down the rocky slopes, then wind quietly through the wide fields below. Tall pines have sprung up at places where the oaks have been destroyed by fire or ax, and sycamores and river birches still stand tall along the creeks of the bottomlands.

But it is the oak-hickory forest of these North Carolina hills that, like the rocks beneath it, impresses with its strength and durability. For seven thousand years it has been the dominant established forest of the granite uplands at Chapel Hill, on which a little less than two hundred years ago the town and the university were built. It is a forest adjusted to a mild climate in which zero temperatures and snowfall are rare or short-lasting, a place where the summer growing season is two hundred days or more, and where the heat under a blazing sun in any month from June to September may sometimes rise to 100°. It is a lovely flowering land, but at times a parched land or one of great downpourings of rain. In summer, severe electrical storms and gale winds tear at its forest trees; in winter, their branches may bow with an unbearable load of ice. But in the long, long ages, the land and its forests were little changed, until the people came.

I would like to have seen this North Carolina wilderness before the American Revolution, when Mark Morgan, Baptist and Welsh-American from Pennsylvania, came there to build a home by the creek that was to bear his name. Morgan's Creek they called it, honoring the man and the landowner, but it is Morgan Creek on maps today, suggesting our passion for change and the corruptions of passing time. But when Mark Morgan and his wife arrived, with their household goods piled on an ox-drawn sled, the creek had no name unless it was one known to the Indians who had been there before him. He had come southward, like his neighbors, on the great wagon trail through Maryland and Virginia, and into North Carolina on the last tide of immigration of Welsh, Scotch, and Scotch-Irish that had been steadily flowing into the South. And, like his companions, Mark Morgan came in search of a peaceful home in the wilderness, to a tract of land he had bought from the Earl of Granville, away from the warring Indians and French in the countries bordering the Allegheny and Monongahela. Until he could build a cabin from the surrounding forest, he and his wife lived by his creek in the hollow trunk of a tall sycamore, ten or twelve feet across. One hundred years later, there were still men who remembered these giant trees along Morgan's Creek, but now the men and the trees and the memories are gone.

There is sadness for a naturalist looking back to Mark Morgan's time, for his primeval land held an aggregation of animals such as one shall never see in these North Carolina woods again. There were many deer in the forests, black bears, and great flocks of wild turkeys with little fear of man. The turkeys fed on the acorns of the dominant oaks—the post oak, white oak, and black oak—and the fruits of the flowering dogwood and other plants of the oak-hickory forest. Perhaps wild turkeys were more numerous then than at any time in North Carolina history. Wolves, cougars, and bobcats ranged the almost unbroken woods, and in their hunger, kept the deer population within the limits of its forest food supply.

And when the deer were scarce or not
easy to kill, the predators preyed on
raccoons, opossums, the little gray foxes,
and the gray squirrel, millions of whose
descendants still live on this land. Now
most of the deer by Morgan Creek
have gone, and even before them,
the black bears, wolves, and cougars disappeared from the great
oak-hickory forest.

It is certain that at times, flocks
of the small green Carolina parakeets, with brilliant red and
yellow heads, flew screaming
through the tops of the creekside
sycamores, whose seeds they fa-
vored, or descended to the apple orchards
of the first settlers and ruined their crops of precious fruit. The
parakeets are gone now, extinct since the early part of this century.

In autumn, Mark Morgan might have seen flocks of migrating
passenger pigeons pour like smoke out of the skies and settle in
the trees of these North Carolina forests. So vast were their numbers that their combined weight broke the limbs of the sturdy oaks
and especially those of the more brittle pines. But Mark Morgan, a
farmer who was to become a distinguished member of his community, was not a journal-keeping man, and he has left us no record.
Some of the early settlers wrote that when they turned their hogs
out into the forest for fattening on the acorns, often there were

none because the great pigeon flocks had been there before them. Now the wild pigeons, too, are gone, and not one has been seen in this North Carolina country since 1894.

It is not difficult to follow Mark Morgan's probable career on the land. Like other explorers and settlers, he had not gone to the wilderness to farm, but to make a home. In the beginning, he must have destroyed the forest by his creek only to keep from starving. The Indians had worked out the best way to break the ground with the least labor—and with only their crude tools, the stone ax and the mattock.

To raise simple food crops, choose the level parts of the forested land, which usually meant the low land not far from the creek. Girdle the giant trees to kill them and never mind the stumps. In a few years, winds and great storms would fell them, for the deadened trunks and roots rotted rapidly in the moist, hot summers. Burn the brush and leaves, and with a stick or a hoe dig between the dead trees and plant in little hills the Indian's corn, beans, and squash. And when the stump fields were no longer fertile, go to another part of the woods, cut the trees, and begin again.

Gather chestnuts, pecans, acorns, and hickory nuts from the forest, and berries and Jerusalem artichokes from the woods borders. For meat, shoot the deer, the turkeys, the squirrels, and opossums. Trap the muskrats, the raccoons, and the otters and use their hides for warm clothing. Seine the creek for fishes, for the sweet flesh of the warmouth, the golden shiner, and the sucker. The fishes are gone now. Like the otters that fed upon them, they were driven from Morgan's Creek, in our own times, by deadly sewage pollution.

This was the pattern of the early settler's life in our eastern forests, and of the first cultivation of some of Mark Morgan's thousands of acres of Carolina land. He was one of several large landowners of this region, and his unbroken forest property lay from his flatlands north of his creek, south to the oak-hickory forest on Laurel Hill. On the northwest, it reached to the rocky promontory on which the University of North Carolina and the village, later called Chapel Hill, would be built.

Mark Morgan's clearings and the mere presence of men on the land had a remarkable effect on the wildlife of his wilderness farm. We need not to have been there to know what went on— the shifting scenes that followed. Animals and plants respond strikingly to changes in uses of the land.

As parts of the great forest disappeared, and hunters and hunting increased, the larger game animals and the big carnivores moved farther away into the deeper woods. With more and larger clearings in the forest, the smaller game and songbirds that love the land under an open sky came and multiplied. New and different plants that cannot live in the densely shaded forest, but only at its borders, arrived first. And when the bobwhite quail—the "partridges" of the settlers—the meadowlarks, and cottontail rabbits, followed, they found more places to nest and more foods in the weeds and grasses of these first fields.

We do not know when Mark Morgan began to change from his simple subsistence farming to the larger fields of a colonial plantation, but it must have been with the spread of tobacco growing and the discovery that cotton would grow on these Southern lands. We do know that he prospered and became a distinguished man in his community and that he was one of ten landowners who gave, collectively, more than a thousand forested acres to establish in 1792 the upland site of the University of North Carolina and the village later called Chapel Hill. And when he died, his estate went to his sons, John and Solomon, of whom Solomon remained on his acres close by Morgan's Creek.

The search for human history is as absorbing as the search for natural history. I am interested in men as well as in the land they occupy and share with its wild things. What a man does to his land determines the destiny of the wildlife on it just as surely as it determines his own. And the concern of the hundreds of farmers I have known in my lifetime for the wild things of their acres has shown me that they care, simply for the pleasure of seeing and hearing the dove, the deer, and the quail from day to day.

There is no record of what Solomon Morgan may have done to his plantation, but he must have continued the land practices of his father. He became a man of prominence in his neighborhood and a justice of the peace. He married Nancy Sears, and of their many children only Jones Morgan and Mary Elizabeth Morgan survived. And when Solomon died in 1847, he was buried just south of Morgan's Creek under three giant hackberry trees that still shelter his grave and those of his

family who lie with him there. These were the last of the pioneering Morgans, and they sleep in their lands by a field that still yields a crop as it did in Mark's and Solomon's day.

e? The Mason Farm, or Mason Plantation, began in 1854. It was on the day that Mary Elizabeth Morgan, only surviving daughter of Solomon, married the Reverend James Pleasant Mason, a Baptist minister, born and reared in Orange County, not far from Chapel Hill. There is no record of when they met—the bright, inquisitive man educated at Wake Forest, and the slender woman with the hauntingly sad face that I saw in an old family photograph. He was twenty-seven and she was twenty-nine, and in their forty years together she was to outlive him by only thirteen months.

From the beginning, if I can judge from his diaries, it was the farm that most concerned the Reverend—the farm quite as much as his preaching and almost as much as his devotion to his family. He and Mary took up their lives together on her share of the Morgan lands in the old gray farmhouse a little way northwest of Morgan Creek. The house stood on an elm-shaded knoll, a site on which the Morgan family had lived for two generations. The Masons had four daughters of whom two died in infancy, and to the surviving girls, Martha James and Varina Caroline, they devoted the next twenty years or more of their lives. Mrs. Cornelia Phillips Spencer, of Chapel Hill, who knew the Mason daughters, wrote of them in the *University of North Carolina Magazine* of February 1895—

From the winter of 1869–70, I saw these girls daily for five years teaching them with my own daughter the beginning of a good education. They soon learned to love reading and to explore for hid treasures in other languages than their own. They finished their school days at the Baptist Female Institute in Raleigh. Their lives at home for a few short years were ideal in relation to their parents and to their intimate associates.

The old family slaves had mostly clung to the old plantation, and, to their "young mistisses," as they called them. Neither of these girls would hesitate to take a long walk to secure for a friend a perfect specimen of some rare wild flower, the fringed gentian, the sabbatia, or the fragrant wintergreen. These walks, these wild woods, the rushing stream and the yellow jessamine that hung over it were among their best teachers and friends.

On September 6, 1881, Varina Caroline, the younger, died of typhoid fever in her twentieth year. On the night before her death her father wrote in his diary the agonized words: "The most dreadful night of my life." On September 6: "At day's dawn *Varina died.* Buried at 5 p.m. N. B. Cobb preached her funeral. She was born June 22, Saturday, 1861."

Two months later, on November 4, 1881, the Reverend Mason wrote: "Dr. Harris came at night . . . Mattie [Martha] quite sick." Saturday, November 5: "Mattie worse. Dr. Harris came this evening and stayed 17 nights in succession."

There were no entries in the Reverend Mason's diary from November 15 to November 22, 1881. Then he wrote: "Mattie died 1 a.m. Mattie born October 16, 1857." Death had come to his older daughter in her twenty-fourth year.

In the small memoranda pages at the end of his diary for 1881, the Reverend Mason wrote: "Many deaths especially from typhoid fever. My children both died . . ." On January 1, 1882: "Snowing this morning everything covered. The Lord be praised for sparing me so long. I don't wish to peer into the future. But as my days may my strength be . . . Not much will."

ﻭﻩ The Reverend James Pleasant Mason lived on for another twelve years, a man broken in health who, himself, survived typhoid fever but was never completely well again. He died June 24, 1893, in his sixty-sixth year; his wife, Mary Elizabeth, died July 17, 1894, in her sixty-ninth year. In her will and that of her husband, drawn up ten years before, the eight-hundred-acre Mason Plantation and $1,000 were bequeathed to the University of North Carolina in the names of their daughters.

There were two conditions in Mrs. Mason's will: that $15.00 a year should be spent to keep up the little Mason Family graveyard, which lies under the cedar trees just southeast of the site of the old Mason homestead, now occupied by the clubhouse of the university's golf course; and that portraits of the girls and their father should be painted from the old family photographs and hung within the halls of the university.

ﻭﻩ For more than fifty years after the deaths of the Masons, there were little changes in the old farm. The university leased the open lands to tenant farmers who worked in the fields. Then, in the late 1940's, a Raleigh business man, Albert Earle Finley, as a gift to the university, built a golf course on two hundred acres of the northern part of the farm. Workmen tore down the Mason home under the elms and in its place built a clubhouse. Green fairways replaced the old fields and some woodlands were cut to open up the course.

Perhaps these changes had little total effect on the wild things that lived there because those birds evicted from the tall-grass fields were replaced by the robins, the mockingbirds, and the blackbirds that love to rove over the green turf searching for earthworms and the insects of the short fairway grass. Cottontail rabbits still came out of the woods to play along the edges of the fairways; great horned owls and foxes hunted them by night, red-tailed hawks by day. Even a big pileated woodpecker came from the nearby woods and slept each night in a hollow of one of the old elms that shade the clubhouse. Bobwhite quail nested in the woods' borders along the edges of the fairways, but their old weedy fields, in which they best loved to nest, were gone. With the disappearance of the tall grasses and shrubs of the older fields, away went the indigo buntings, the blue grosbeaks, and the song and field sparrows, the yellowthroats, and the chats.

If you want to find them now, go down the yellow road in summer, eastward, past Finley Golf Course Clubhouse and the pathetic little Mason graveyard under the cedar grove. Walk beyond the cemetery plot on the earth road through the splendid tall pines and sycamores, the sweet gums and oaks that still grow along the north side of Morgan Creek.

Go past the woods to the break in the trees, to the concrete dam that spans the creek. There you can cross the stream and see as I did, on my first visit to the farm, the sweep of the fields, the wide woodlands and open sky. There on the last six hundred wild acres of the old Mason Farm, in its southeast part, you will find the indigo buntings, the blue grosbeaks, and the quail, the red cardinal flocks of hundreds in the rose hedges and in the weedy borders of the old fields. There you will see the last of the Morgan and Mason land, as it was in their day, with the hooting of owls and a glimpse of foxes and raccoons that run over the old roads in the night. In the soft April dusk, you can still hear the first whippoor-wills of the year calling there, just as the Reverend Mason heard them and noted them down in his diaries of a century that has passed. This is a land where the fields and woods are in balance and the numbers and varieties of its wild things reach their richest and fullest expression.

As I write this, the land and its animals are safe by the grace of the university that has kept this part of the Mason Farm a wild refuge, a place where students of plants and animals can continue their research. Perhaps it will stay as it is for generations of young naturalists to discover its hidden places and to know its wild loneliness and sweep of fields, forests, and sky. It is with the hope that the farm will remain unchanged that I have told the stories of some of its occupants and of those wildlings that, once evicted by too much human invasion, cannot come back. It is with joy that I have written of a land so quiet, so undisturbed that the wood duck and the wild turkey still live there, along with the mink and muskrats of Morgan Creek and the hawks and owls of Laurel Hill.

January

≪ January is hope on the old Mason Farm, and you can sense it when you walk there. The long, brilliantly starred cold nights of December, and its short dark days, are past. The arc of the sun is higher in the south. Its warm yellow light melts the snow until it lies in blue pools across the fallow fields under a vast cup of sky. In Big Oak Woods and in Siler's Bog, beneath the black-trunked trees, the amber lagoons by Yancey Brook grow longer, fed by the icy snow water. From the temporary pools in the old fields, I hear the first faint calls of the chorus frogs. Their day is coming and they seem to know it, but their frog voices are muted by the sharp wind that still blows bitter across the land.

By mid-January, the first bird songs, sweet with the promise of spring, lift up out of the rose hedges—from cardinals, towhees, mockingbirds, song, and fox, sparrows. In Big Oak Woods, the white-breasted nuthatch pipes his nasal penny-trumpet notes, and the tufted titmouse begins to sing. Snows and cold are still to come, but the birds feel the lengthening days and the increased light that, by its magic, starts the spring and summer cycle of their mating time. And the songs that come from each bird's throat are the first faint stirrings of its breeding season, yet two months away.

Now the crows fly wild over the land. They rise in black flocks from last summer's fields of corn and whirl away on the wind with a great outpouring of caws and guttural cries. I think I hear joy in their shoutings, and sometimes I see them draw tighter together as though swarming about some hapless hawk in their midst. But when the flock opens with a wild flutter of wings, there is no hawk there, for the big red-tails, their favorite targets of attack, have not yet returned to Laurel Hill. The crows turn back from their westward flight over the woods and move in a black mass toward a distant grassy field. I hear their cries, suddenly higher, louder, and exultant, as they swoop downward and follow the field's edge. I suspect they have seen a red or a gray fox and that they will revile it until it runs away and disappears in Willow Oak Swamp to the east.

Then come the mild days of the January thaw, sometime about the third week in the month. Clouds of midges suddenly appear from their hiding places and hang in the bright sunshine over the muddy roads of the old farm. Hundreds of the gauzy-winged creatures dance up and down or float like dust motes in the soft yellow light. Beyond them, as in a dream world, I see the brown of the leaves on the floor of Big Oak Woods, the black trunks of the trees, the deep green of needled pine branches. In the night, the foxes bark shrilly; and walking the old roads by day, I find their twisted scats and their tracks in the soft mud. They are not yet breeding, but soon the vixens will be in their heat.

CHAPTER II

Trail of the Little Gray Ghost

That cold February morning, I had walked five miles over the snowy fields of the Mason Farm and through black-trunked woods before the trails of the gray foxes had ended. It was a day to remember. A naturalist feels lucky when a light, wet snow enables him to follow a single fox trail to its conclusion. That morning I had followed not one, but two of them. Something within the foxes themselves—something that had driven them part way through the night—had made this possible.

During the summer, after dark in the glare of my powered lamp, I had seen live foxes on the old farm roads. But the light had scarcely touched them before they were gone—ghosts slipping into the shadows of the woods trails without a whisper of sound.

I did not need to see them now. From their tracks I could read their stories, told in a language that only one who, in his heart, runs with the fox and the wind, can interpret with true understanding. For to know a wild thing is to be touched with its own magic awareness of earth and sky—to know its fire or fear, its loneliness or joy, its need to satisfy a thousand urges.

Ahead, the rising sun had sparkled a blaze of light from the snow's surface. A golden sun trail lay across the wide fields from the dark trees of Big Oak Woods, a quarter of a mile away to the nearby banks of Morgan Creek. Under the streamside thickets, the pointed tracks of cottontail rabbits crisscrossed until, in places, the snow lay packed under their trails. The wind, sweeping the icy creek, was cold and sweet.

I had come on the trails of two gray foxes after crossing the concrete bridge and had followed them over the white, buried road that led across the North Carolina farm. Each separate trail was etched in the snow as sharply as that of a small dog in fresh concrete. Where the trail of the wider-chested dog might have shown all four feet in two parallel lines of travel, the fox trail was a single line, as if only one paw had touched the snow. The reddish feet of the narrower-chested fox were swung ahead in an almost straight line and each hind foot laid so exactly in the 1½-inch-long foretrack that only a single trail showed where each had passed.

꒰ The gray fox lives throughout most of the United States, except in the Great Plains and Rocky Mountain states. There are forms or varieties that vary in size and color—the western gray fox, the desert gray fox, the northern gray fox, the southern gray fox, and others.

Weighing only about seven pounds, the southern gray fox is smaller than the better-known red fox. Its grizzled, salt-and-pepper-gray body, with rusty red along the sides and neck, is about two feet long; the black-tipped bushy gray tail, with a black streak along its top, adds another twelve or fourteen inches to the fox's length. He stands not much more than a foot above the ground at the shoulders, and when he trots, his paw marks along his trail are about eleven inches apart.

The character of this small wild dog is a mixture of raccoon, bobcat, squirrel, and even of cottontail rabbit. He will fight desperately against overwhelming odds. And he will leap into the lower branches of a tree and, with the scrambling aid of his four sharp claws on each foot, jump upward from limb to limb as surefootedly as a squirrel or cat. He loves also the refuge of the densest thickets, the thorniest brier patches, and the roughest rock piles.

The gray fox has a streak of curiosity that despite his wildness and caution sometimes leads him to his death. Hunters whom I know take advantage of the gray fox by using a predator call—a small wooden device through which the hunter blows to produce the simulated squeal of a rabbit. Gray foxes, which are fond of eating rabbits when they can catch them, are lured to these calls and come unerringly to the source of the sound. Many of them are shot by the hidden hunter. Foxes will also come to the mimicked calls of a crow in distress.

Years ago, Dr. Alexander Wetmore, then Secretary of the Smithsonian Institution, told me about a gray fox's curiosity that ended comically, and not tragically. He and Watson Perrygo, a preparator of the United States Museum, were in the Blue Ridge Mountains of Virginia, not far from Washington, D.C., to shoot some crows for the Museum's collections. Dr. Wetmore had squatted under the downsweeping branches of a wild apple tree. He was blowing on a crow call to attract crows while Perrygo hid with his gun behind an old stone wall. Both were astonished when a gray fox, responding to Dr. Wetmore's crow call, suddenly dashed toward his hiding place. But in doing so, the fox first leaped upon the back of Perrygo in order to clear the stone wall.

"It was a question," Dr. Wetmore said, "of who was the most surprised—Watson or the fox!"

A gray fox is not so swift as the longer-legged, black-footed red fox of open country. To escape from dogs that hunt him in his woodland home, he depends more on trail tricks—leaping to the top of a rail fence and running agilely along it to throw the dogs off his scent; or climbing a tree, then running out on its longest branch and leaping to the ground. While the dogs are still puzzling over the broken trail, the gray fox may be two miles away. If pressed too closely he may hide in a wood pile or rock crevice rather than run cross-country for fifteen, twenty, or even fifty miles as a pursued red fox will.

A gray fox will also shin up the vertical trunk of a tree, like a small boy, and hide in its leafiest branches or in the abandoned nest of a hawk or crow, if the dogs chase him too hotly. Yet I was to learn that even a tree is not always a refuge for a gray fox, that —sometimes—it can be a deadly trap.

From the two sets of tracks in the snow, I could see that the foxes had been traveling side by side. The paw marks of one, possibly the slightly larger male, were only a little bigger than those of the other. It was mating time and in places the tracks ran wildly ahead like those of two playful dogs. The trails told how they had raced in the night, their short legs propelling their small gray bodies, their bushy tails flowing behind them. The sharp, eager faces, with their large, luminous eyes and big ears had pointed southward, their short muzzles with brown streaks—like the dark masks of raccoons—raised slightly into the night.

The gray fox is more nocturnal than the red, its eyes better adapted to the dark. At dusk, the pupils become rounded in the subdued light, adjusting to the growing blackness of oncoming night. But the gray fox also hunts in the daytime. At dawn, as the light increases, the pupils contract with the growing brilliance of the day until the vertical slits screen out the brightness. At noon one summer day, a gray fox sped across a Southern road in front of my car and whisked into a pine woods like a gray wraith. Gray foxes often hunt well into the morning and may start their night's hunt in the late afternoon, especially when there are young to be fed.

Once, where the pair of gray foxes I was following had stopped, a yellow stain spread across the snow. The scent of urine came to me strongly, a catlike odor that had lingered on the clear cold air. These urinating places of the gray foxes are of great interest to foxes that come along the trail later. They are thought to be scent stations, or communication centers where foxes sift through their sharp little minds the shades of meaning in every individual odor.

For a time, the trails ran straight ahead over the snow-hidden road, not deviating like those of foxes on the hunt. When hungry, a fox will wander across open fields and back to woodlands and swamps again. In ten thousand hidden places a lone gray fox may scent delicate and delicious odors of bird, rabbit, or mouse rising from pine, greenbrier, and wild blackberry thickets, from rose hedges, cattail marshes, and thick patches of weeds and grasses in old fields. For there the cottontail rabbit has its resting place, the mouse its nest, the mockingbird its nightly roost.

At dawn one misty autumn day, after I had spent the night in the woods, I watched a gray fox steal with lowered belly across a grassy field. He held his head high, swinging his moist, sensitive black nose from side to side like a pointer or setter dog, testing every subtle current of air. Suddenly he crouched before a clump of tawny grasses. Then he leaped forward in a catlike spring. A covey of brown quail roared up from the place where they had roosted for the night. The fox bounded high with them and snatched one out of the air. With the dead bird gripped in his jaws, he trotted away and disappeared in a deep, dry drainage ditch.

ꝓ Some naturalists believe that gray foxes remain paired all of their lives, or until one is killed. Yet, even if this were true, it is fox nature that, once a year, the union must be plighted again. In the South, it is under the bright stars of mid-February that the first vixens come into their heat. Then the short, sharp barks of the mated pairs, like the yapping of feisty dogs, pierce the winter cold.

Mating and pregnancies continue through March, and by April and May many vixens are nursing their young. But even in June, I have heard the barking of pairs in the low Carolina hills. Then, for a month or two, there may be fox silence until autumn when the eerie night squalling of the young begins. Once, on a starlit September night, while I listened to flying squirrels harvesting hickory nuts in a nearby tree, a young fox squalled so close to me that my hair stood on end. Only a young horned owl can outdo the gray fox's demoniac night sounds.

🐾 I had not suspected that the snow trail of the paired foxes I was following would lead me to the home den. Gray foxes have several winter dens for resting and undisturbed sleeping. North Carolina fox hunters had told me that, when their hounds chased gray foxes too closely in the woods, the foxes often took refuge under the great mounds of slab wood left by old sawmill operations. One hunter showed me an immense pile of sawdust near an old mill site. It was riddled with burrows dug by red foxes. A gray fox, he said, seldom if ever digs its own burrow. In some of these abandoned red fox dens the vixen gray fox bears her one to seven young, usually four in a litter and one litter a year.

Some of the dens are under old buildings in lonely forest clearings, others in rock crevices in the hills, in hollow logs or trees in forests of oak, hickory, and pine, or in low woods of swamp maple. I learned that, for some reason known only to the foxes, their dens are seldom far from water—a swamp pond, woodland lake, or winding creek.

A farmer I knew of had raised a dark-colored gray fox of great courage and alertness that he called Perro. Perro drank water mostly at night, between ten and two in the morning, when wild gray foxes are most active, and during another active gray fox period, from six to seven in the morning. He could race up a five-foot ladder in his pen, leap six feet or more, and preferred to sleep outside his nest box except during the coldest or rainiest times. He slept soundly most of the day, but awakened at the slightest unusual sound that touched his wonderfully keen ears— the distant barking of a dog, a car starting, or the whistle of a diesel engine far down the valley.

When he was four months old, Perro was full-grown: he weighed seven pounds and nine ounces. He liked to play with the farmer's dog and was still playful when he was ten months old. When Perro was very young, he would creep on his belly to the dog, wagging his tail from side to side. Then he would nuzzle the old dog's breasts and try to nurse.

At fourteen months, the farmer gave Perro his freedom. The first day that he ran free he got into trouble. Used to dogs, he had gone to a neighboring farm, where he was attacked by the farmer's chow dog. Perro, in a slashing defense, had beaten the chow thoroughly. He came home only a few times after that. Then he was gone, returned to the wild, free life that the farmer had generously given back to him.

◡ ℮ᴈ Tracks in the snow tell much of the news about a wild animal. One has only to follow them to read the animal's winter story. Hunger must have touched the mated gray foxes I was following, for after a mile of travel, the two trails separated. Sometimes paired foxes hunt together, but more often they are said to hunt alone.

Where the trails forked at Big Oak Woods, I was left with a choice. I chose to follow the larger tracks of the one I suspected was the male. His trail went not across the whitened fields, but through snow-filled woods. A crow flying high overhead called a sharp warning of my approach, and a gray squirrel barked from a giant oak ahead. The snow piled on twigs of dogwood, holly, and chinquapin, brushed against my arms and face and sifted down on the blue-white surface. A cardinal whistled a morning song, then flashed red in flight as his wings *thrupped* on the cold air.

The fox trail wound between the trees ahead, avoiding the thorny tangles of greenbrier, yet stopping by them as though the fox had paused to sniff the air. Then the trail moved on southward. Suddenly the tracks stopped and turned toward a dense honeysuckle thicket. As they approached it, they were closer together. Apparently the fox had slowed his pace. A deep gash in the snow that had torn up the leaves showed that he had leaped and turned sharply around a thicket. A rabbit's trail led away in great eight-foot bounds, the fox's tracks following for a little way. Then the trail of the fox again turned toward the south.

Under a gray-barked white oak the fox had stopped to dig in the snow. A few crunched bits of an acorn lay on the surface at the place where he had chewed the dry but nourishing seed. Farther on, by the side of a moldering log, the fox had paused. A quick, short leap over the log and a few drops of blood on the snow told me that he had caught and gulped a woodland mouse.

To hunt in the open is to risk life for any small wild creature. The gray fox himself might tremble at the strong scent of the bobcat whose tracks I had seen in a nearby swamp. In a fight, the gray fox could best a domestic cat but not the larger, heavier wild cat, which sometimes kills and eats foxes. In California, a naturalist had seen a golden eagle sweep down in a terrifying dive to drive its talons deep into a gray fox sleeping on a high rock in the sun. He had shuddered at the almost human screams of the dying animal as it fought to free itself from the eagle's deadly grip.

Most of all, the gray fox has reason to fear Man, with his dogs and guns. As I followed the fox's trail, I remembered the hatred that men who hunt wild turkeys hold for the gray fox. In a small country store where I had queried about foxes, a fierce-looking little man had said: "You want foxes? Just come over my way where they's so thick they've cleaned out all my rabbits and wild turkeys. I hate the damn foxes. If there'd be a way I could touch one trigger and blow 'em all to hell, I'd do it!"

Another told of a gray fox his dogs had chased so hotly that, to escape, it had climbed straight up the vertical trunk of a tree. It had reached the first horizontal branch thirty feet up when the turkey hunter arrived. When the fox tried to hide close to the trunk, the hunter had shot it to the ground. Although a fox may find safety in a tree from a dog, or from its ancient enemy the wolf, it may meet certain death there when the enemy is a man with a gun.

The turkey hunter's hatred is unjustified, even though foxes try to catch turkeys. The big, twelve- to twenty-pound birds are the wildest and wariest of any in the woods, as any turkey hunter knows. Their keenness of hearing and sight matches, or even excels, that of a fox. In studies of the food habits of foxes throughout the year over the best wild turkey country, scientists discovered that birds of all kinds eaten by foxes were a small fraction of their diet. Most red and gray foxes eat cottontail rabbits, deer mice and meadow mice, wild fruit, and beechnuts.

◦ The fox trail I was following had swung sharply to the east. Perhaps the wind had shifted in the night and forced the fox to circle in order for him to scent whatever prey had been ahead. His move had been a significant one as I was soon to discover.

A gray fox has forty-two teeth, the same number as those of the red fox, arctic foxes, wolf, coyote, and bears. One day I found the bleached skull of a fox lying on the nearby wooded slopes of Laurel Hill. It had twenty teeth in the upper jaw; twenty-two in the lower (two extra molars). It had incisors, or cutting teeth, like those of a dog and long canines for catching and holding its prey or for fighting. These are the long, pointed teeth that a dog shows when it snarls. The skull also had premolars and molars that the animal had used for grinding and chewing. This is why a gray fox can catch and hold a struggling rabbit, chew meat or grind up bones, gnaw the hardest nut into edible pieces, eat fresh corn from a field, pick up grasshoppers, crickets, beetles and the caterpillars of butterflies and moths, or delicately pluck ripe persimmons, apples, or grapes from a tree or vine.

But if the teeth of a gray fox serve it well, its cocked ears and moist black nose are among the sharpest in nature. The trail of the fox I was following had approached the south edge of Big Oak Woods. After circling widely, it had turned abruptly to intercept the trail of a wild turkey. The distance between each footprint of the bird told me that it had been striding swiftly as it fed. Each track was more than four inches from heel to the point of the longest middle toe, which told me that it was a very large gobbler. In places I saw that the small flock, which often fed in these woods, had been scratching for acorns under the snow. All the turkey trails suddenly moved in long strides toward the wood's edge. Then they disappeared as the turkeys took to the air. Early that morning the gray fox had stalked the largest one, probably the gobbler, and had followed its trail, quite likely with his black nose close to the snow.

The keen nose of a fox or of a dog must have a certain moisture for it to assimilate the scent-trail particles. A fox's sense of smell is made keen by delicate nerve endings and tissues which hold the odorous substances that pass over them from the air or from the ground. No man with his dull sense of smell can appreciate the world of odors in which, and by which, a wild fox lives.

The fox's trail showed its careful stalk of the turkey. Crouching

low, it had crept from thicket to thicket, keeping a large tree between it and the feeding gobbler. Deep marks in the snow behind the tree showed that it had leaped around the trunk; its trail leading straight ahead, that it had bounded swiftly at the gobbler.

How fast is the rush of a fox at its prey? In an automobile I once timed a gray fox, running full speed, at thirty-five miles an hour; this one must have been running that fast. But swift as it was, its rush came too late. The turkey's trail ended just ahead of the fox's. There must have been a thunderous beating of wings as the gobbler left the ground with the rest of the flock to fly out of Big Oak Woods. Beyond an open field, on the lower slopes of Laurel Hill, hundreds of yards away, I saw the marks in the snow where the flock had alighted. There, far from the wistful little fox at the edge of Big Oak Woods, they had resumed their feeding.

Now the fox's trail turned eastward, across a field and into a swamp. I had expected the tracks of the pair of gray foxes to rejoin there, but the single trail went on through the swamp in places where the trunks of young sweet gums grew so densely I could scarcely pass. The fox seemed to have grown more cautious, for his steps were shorter. He had stopped more often, perhaps to scent the wind.

When the fox trail ended at the base of a leaning sycamore near Morgan Creek, my heart leaped. The fox had scrambled up the white, leaning trunk. I looked up into the bare branches half expecting to see him crouched in a fork, basking in the sun. A few clusters of brown leaves still clung to the windfallen tree. It was among these that I searched carefully. As I moved under the trunk of the tree toward its tip, I saw from deep marks in the snow that the fox had leaped to the ground. Perhaps he had broken his scent trail deliberately.

Where Willow Oak Swamp touched Morgan Creek, the fox trail crossed the stream over a fallen tree that bridged the water. One hundred yards beyond the creek, I found the den. The tracks of the fox entered an eight-inch hole near what had been the top of a giant willow oak that, years before, had crashed to the floor of the swamp. The old log was hollow and undoubtedly had a roomy chamber within its large base. Here the tracks of the vixen had come in from the northeast and had also disappeared in the hole.

In April, when purple violets covered the banks of Morgan Creek and bees droned at the pink-white flowers of wild apple, I returned to the den. There were no foxes about, but I heard the faint growls of young ones quarreling within. As they grew older they would become more sociable and even show an attachment for each other.

e3 In June, when wild swamp roses were in flower, I went there again. All about the den lay the playthings of the young foxes— discarded bones and furry feet of rabbits that the young foxes chew and toss in the air as puppies worry an old shoe. At the end of summer, when full-grown, they would travel on their individual ways, far from Willow Oak Swamp and the thicketed banks of Morgan Creek.

I told no one about the den, remembering the hatred of hunters for the gray ghost. But I also remembered a kindly farmer who had given a gray fox his freedom. More than that, I was thinking of the rabbit and the turkeys that had gotten away from the fox that day and the whole fabric of life on this farm that is bound up, so intricately, one life with another.

I had seen that where turkeys and foxes forage, the hunger of each would see that not all acorns grow into oaks. And the fox would be sure in his hungry way that mice and rabbits would not overrun the earth. I had learned that where the gray fox runs, his life might touch, even if ever so lightly, on the delicate destinies of butterflies, beetles, and moths; and that the hungry bobcat or eagle will see, in turn, the gray fox stretched lifeless on the ground.

In February:
Before Spring

It is one mile, from the den of the gray foxes I found that winter day in Willow Oak Swamp, westward across the fields of the Mason Farm to Laurel Hill Woods. But it is three weeks in time, from early February to March, before I see turkey vultures that have come back for the year's nesting, soaring commonly over the wooded hill. There one can see all that is left of some of the dwellings of tenant farmers who worked the land. In lonely clearings, a few are naked cellars, open to the sky; others have timbered walls still standing that were cabins and tobacco barns at fields' edges. Now, fifty years later, they are within the oak woodland that has reclaimed the lower slopes of Laurel Hill. With the people gone, red foxes dug their burrows under the old buildings and turkey vultures came through the open windows to raise their young on the earthen floors of the few cabins that remain.

In late February, the Mason Farm is between winter and spring, before the tide of bird migration sweeps northward with its fanfare of wings and song. The sunshine is warm and the fields lie mostly bare. There are few winters, late in this second month of the year, when I see more than a light whirling of snow that scarcely whitens the earth and the floor of the dark woods. Then, within a day, it is gone. But the cold is bitter at twenty degrees, and I dress warmly to walk this freezing and thawing land.

Near February's end, the great horned owls have begun their nesting and boom their cries in the night. Mourning

doves coo softly from the woods by day, then fly like gray
arrows, their wings whistling over the fields. Along Morgan
Creek, I see the tracks of a raccoon that has come out to hunt
during one of the slowly warming nights. In sunny places
along the stream, protected by thickets from the wind,
robins, bright in their new spring plumage, feed along the
creek's edge. The promise is there, a little stronger, and
to find it, I hunt along the waterways.

CHAPTER III

How a Vulture Finds Its Prey

ॐ In March the Carolina winds blow wildest over the naked sleeping fields, then moan through leafless Big Oak Woods with the sound of a rushing train. For days, Morgan Creek, swollen and muddy from fields washed by the spring deluge, roars like a giant. The placid stream of winter, now yellowed and transformed, rises above its banks, tearing at the groves of sycamores and river birches that mark its course through the low-hill country. It is a time, while the fields lie sodden under stormy March skies, that the big black turkey vultures return to the old Mason Farm at Chapel Hill.

All that winter of my first year in the South I had seen one, perhaps two, searching day after day for the winter-killed wild things. I knew of two deer and a few opossums that a pack of dogs had slaughtered on the slopes of Laurel Hill. And there were the frozen carcasses of raccoons, rabbits, squirrels, wild turkeys, and quail, wounded by the hunters' guns, that had crawled to hidden places to die. Some of them, shot just before an early winter storm, lay covered by the first fall of snow.

It had seemed strange to see vultures in low hunting flights over the white fields and woodlands. In the North, one links them always with the green fields of summer.

The few wintering vultures had been joined by others—perhaps migrants moving northward as the sun rose higher each day and the snows retreated. More and more groups of them rode the wild March winds, sweeping low over the flatlands, then rising to clear the treetops, now dipping again to skim the wide fields in a ceaseless daytime hunt for food.

How do the turkey vultures find these winter-killed animals? Some scientists have insisted that it is by their sharp eyesight alone; others, that they find their prey by an extraordinarily keen sense of smell. Yet in most of the experiments with them that I had read about, vultures, like many other birds, seemed to have little sense of smell or perhaps none at all.

John James Audubon had experimented with a captive vulture and claimed that it could not smell its food. He was an astute naturalist and a close observer of birds, but when he presented his conclusions in 1826 before a group of scientists in Edinburgh, Scotland, they aroused a controversy that was to continue, unresolved, for more than a hundred years. No one knew, until a long time afterward, that Audubon had probably experimented, not with the turkey vulture but with the Southern black vulture. And apparently no one guessed that there might be a difference in the senses of these two birds.

One ornithologist I knew believed that turkey vultures found their prey by a mysterious occult sense not known to man and not demonstrable in the vultures themselves. He published an article about it in an annual report of the Smithsonian Institution, but his conclusions did not solve the problem to my satisfaction or to that of the many scientists interested in the matter. I had seen evidence that turkey vultures on the Mason Farm had cleaned the bones of winter-killed animals, even in the hidden places. It was a mystery I was to solve, at least to my own satisfaction, on this large university farm.

Now the snows had gone or lay ever so briefly under the strong March sunlight. On Laurel Hill, Christmas ferns lifted their green swords above the brown leaves along every gurgling, rain-filled brook. But on the open flats below, it was in the leafing of the rose hedges, which divided the brown fields, that one saw the first green fire of summer. Then it leaped from the hedges to the blackberry and honeysuckle at the wood's edge in the bursting of a million tiny new leaves.

The fresh smell of water was everywhere, rising from melted snows in the sweet black leaf mold of woods and from downpouring spring rain. For a few weeks this is a land half submerged, belonging neither to the earth nor to the waterways. In the temporary shallow ponds of open fields, thousands of tiny chorus frogs swelled their throats in ratchety mating calls under the warming sun. In the deeper, permanent pools of Willow Oak Swamp, the ducklike clacking of a myriad of wood frogs rang night and day; from every roadside ditch the leopard frogs snored their amphibian cries of spring. Blacksnakes, newly stirred from hibernation, sunned in the forest clearings, and the cooing of mated mourning doves, soft as the caress of the March air, wafted through the wet warming woods.

ఆ The turkey vultures had come back to the Mason Farm that spring of 1961, and with them they had brought me an age-old mystery. That year I made three discoveries, two of which helped prepare me for an experiment in learning how a turkey vulture finds its food.

A vulture's day begins and ends at its roost. Although the turkey vultures I had watched usually hunted alone, they sometimes soared about in small groups. At the end of the day, however, the roost is the social gathering place of all the vultures that hunt for miles around. It is usually in a tall tree projecting above the forest.

Late one March afternoon, I saw turkey vultures soaring in from all directions to a large tree on the slopes of nearby Edwards Mountain. While I watched, nineteen vultures settled in the dead branches of an enormous oak just before the sun set. It was their roosting tree; by watching it I learned of the superb sensitivity of the turkey vulture to the ocean of air in which it spends most of its life and how it has learned to use this to survive.

For years I had known that the turkey vulture was a late riser, but I had never known why. After I discovered the roosting tree, I began to watch it early in the morning, soon after sunrise.

On the mornings of days when the March winds rested, long after the fiery sun had come up over Willow Oak Swamp to the east, I saw the vultures waiting quietly in their roosting tree on

Edwards Mountain. With the
marvelous patience of most
wild things, they perched on
the dead limbs of the old oak,
like feathered ships becalmed in
a sea of still air. In their wisdom, they knew that without the
winds to ride upon, which
make their long daily flights
almost effortless, they must
wait for the rising sun and its
power. For with its heat would
come the thermals that on warm
days can lift a vulture swiftly, without
a wingbeat, a thousand feet into the air. And
so they waited, their wings spread, their
backs turned to the warming sun.

For a while they sat preening and sun-bathing. By ten o'clock
the sun's heat started the first bubbles of warm air eddying upward
from the bare fields. Expanding, the bubbles would rise above the
cooler air of the forest until they were powerful updrafts whirling
into the sky.

The vultures seemed to sense when the rising air was right for
them and the time had come to leave the roosting tree. Now, one
by one, I watched them lean forward, spread their wings, and leap
into the air. After a few starting wingbeats, they glided out over
the forest toward the open fields. There, like eager hounds sniffing
a cold trail, they swung about seeking a column of rising air. I

45

could see the moment when each vulture found a thermal—the sudden wingbeat and sharp, eager turn. Then each bird began to ascend, almost straight upward, spiraling in quick circles on the updraft, as though climbing an aerial stair. When five hundred to a thousand feet in the sky, the vultures turned in different directions to glide across the country. Their daily hunt for food had begun.

Early on a morning in May, I made the two discoveries on the Mason Farm that led to my experiment in learning which of its senses a turkey vulture may use in its hunting. That day I had been following the trail of a raccoon in the dry dust of a road that leads across the farm and around Big Oak Woods. Curious to see what adventures the animal might have had, I followed its trail eagerly. The woods were in full shining leaf, and grasses along the old road were two feet tall. Daisies were beginning to whiten the fields, and wild blackberries in flower were like white smoke in the roadside thickets. The scent of wild honeysuckle, drifting out of Willow Oak Swamp and Big Oak Woods, drenched the air with its sweetness.

In the dry dust, the small, handlike prints of a raccoon showed that it had waddled from one side of the road to the other in its miles of wandering during the previous night. It was not a day to expect death, but in the wild, death waits everywhere for the unwary.

While following the raccoon's trail, I came suddenly on a dead opossum in the grasses at the edge of the road. Its belly had been ripped open and its entrails lay partly on the ground. The tracks of large dogs were concentrated in the dust by the small carcass. During the night, the pack that roams the Mason Farm, living on rabbits and other small game, had surprised the opossum. It had been caught well away from a tree to which it might have fled for safety.

Unlike the gray fox, the opossum has no swiftness of foot with which to escape. A full-grown raccoon might have fought off the dogs or held them at bay, but the smaller, shyer opossum had not a chance against the pack. I dragged its body into the grass and walked on. Then, on the road ahead, I saw the body of a black racer. The snake was dead. I learned later that a farm hand had killed it only the day before. Now I had a plan. I picked up the dead snake, walked back to the dead opossum, and put them in a sack I carry for transporting live snakes home for short periods of captivity while I study their ways.

Nearby, at the edge of Big Oak Woods, I saw a maple tree with a hollow in its trunk a few feet above the ground. I put the bagged dead animals in the hole in the tree, so deeply that I could not see the sack in a recess within the hollow.

The quarry was perfectly hidden. Now to see if a vulture could find it. One hundred yards away, I hid within the depths of a thicket of young pines that covered the banks of a ditch in an open field. From there I could watch the skies all about for an approaching vulture. All that day I watched, but not a vulture came near.

The next morning I hid in the thicket at nine o'clock, about an hour before the vultures usually leave their roost. At eleven, a vulture swept down the field with a light breeze under its tail. It was gliding with the direction of the wind, about one hundred feet above the ground, in a typical, low-altitude hunting flight. When it had traveled, without turning, about two hundred yards past the red maple, I thought it would fly the length of the field and perhaps beyond. But suddenly it dipped one wing, raised the other, and turned in a wide circle. It came back, gliding lower and lower, facing into the wind that was now blowing from the hollow tree to the vulture.

Slowly, with a majestic sweep of its broad black wings, it rose into the air over the maple. It circled twice above the tree, then flew down the field again. When it turned and came back upwind, it glided toward the maple as though drawn to it on a string. Thirty feet from where the dead animals were concealed, the vulture alighted on the ground.

For a while it stood facing the hollow tree. With its head and tail lifted high, it held its long, sharply hooked bill into the wind. Its whole posture was remarkably like that of a setter dog pointing a bird hidden in the grass. Suddenly it ran a few feet and

with heavy, labored flapping, took off. Slowly it circled, then glided down and alighted on a dead limb of the maple tree. My heart was pounding. I was sure now that I had made a major discovery, but I did not know at the time that someone else had been making detailed scientific experiments about turkey vultures that were far more exact than my own.

For twenty-five minutes the bird perched quietly in the tree. When a farm hand, driving a tractor, roared down the road, the frightened vulture flew away. I had proved to my satisfaction, however, that a turkey vulture does locate its food, first by its sense of smell, especially when the animal carcass is concealed, and then by the sharpness of its sight. Had the snake and the opossum been lying in full view at the base of the tree, I am sure that the vulture would have flown down to them.

A long business trip took me away the next day and I did not repeat the test. Three years later, I had complete verification of my experiment from another source, and the long controversy about the turkey vulture, which had extended over one hundred thirty-eight years, ended.

Unknown to me, for twenty-five years Kenneth E. Stager of the Los Angeles County Museum had experimented as I had, by picking up dead animals and hiding them in bushes or hollow trees. Then he hid close by to watch the actions of the turkey vultures that eventually came flying near. In every one of his experiments the vultures approached the hidden bait, with the wind blowing to them from the carcasses. These and other field tests suggested to Stager that one of the vulture's senses, other than sight, aided it in finding dead animals.

To make more exact scientific tests, Stager developed a clever method of wafting the odors of dead animals into the sky by hiding the carcasses in a unit attached to a blower and electric fan. The dead animals on which vultures are accustomed to feeding, Stager gathered from the surrounding countryside—deer, bobcats, and other native animals. To eliminate the possibility of the day-flying vultures' seeing the dead animals, Stager put them in the unit at night. From the large numbers of vultures gathered around the unit on the following days, Stager got conclusive proof that the turkey vulture does find its food—first—by odor.

However, he did not limit his olfactory tests to the American turkey vulture, but tested vultures in India by hiding the carcasses of tigers and other dead animals in places where vultures came regularly. Not one of these so-called Aegyptine (Old World) vultures of that country could detect carrion by its odor.

Stager found from other of his researches and observations in America that the Southern black vulture, with which Audubon had experimented, and the big California condor do not locate their food first by its odor, as the turkey vulture does. Not having this capacity for detecting prey, these two species use the turkey vulture's skill to their advantage by watching it as it floats effortlessly in the skies. If it descends to an animal carcass, they follow it to earth and usually drive it away to have the feast for themselves.

*The Barred
Owls of Big
Oak Woods*

I don't know when the pair of barred owls moved northward out of Siler's Bog to nest in Big Oak Woods. Only the night winds and the stars know of such owl business, all cloaked in the dark. And I could only assume that the owls I discovered in the oak woods were the same pair which had nested for years in a hollow sweet gum in the bog. Barred owls are deeply attached to their nesting places and will not leave them unless forced to. In Siler's Bog one winter day, I found the hollow tree in which they had nested, fallen to the ground. Perhaps a high wind or simply the rotting and eventual weakening of the old trunk had caused it to topple over. It was quite reasonable that the pair of owls, after losing their home, had moved to Big Oak Woods only one thousand feet away.

Later, one March day, while walking in the evening shadows by the east border of Big Oak Woods, I *hoo-ah*'d a guttural imitation of a barred owl's cry, expecting to hear the usual response from the pair in the bog. I was surprised when for the first time I heard a pair of barred owls call from deep in the woods at my back. I turned from the road and walked westward under big oaks and beeches, onward to a grove of tall pines in the center of the tract.

Suddenly a barred owl flew out of the densely needled crown of a pine. After a few slow beats of its broad wings, it floated silently through the tops of the trees and disappeared. Then I saw what I thought was the owl's nest—a large cluster of old sticks and leaves high in the crown of the tree. One year the pair of red-shouldered hawks that usually nested in the tall sycamores along Morgan Creek had built this nest in the pine. Perhaps the hawks had been disturbed by some human wanderer along the creek, but they stayed only one nesting season in Big Oak Woods before moving back to their old site in the sycamore.

Barred owls often take over an abandoned hawk's nest or that of a crow or a gray squirrel. When I rapped on the pine in Big Oak Woods and a barred owl peered over the side of the nest, then settled back out of sight, I was sure that it was one of the pair from Siler's Bog. Each spring this pair had become used to my hammering on their hollow tree to see if they were at home, and after a look at me from the hollow, the owl occupying the nest would draw back within its retreat. This owl had behaved in the same way and made no attempt to fly.

In Big Oak Woods these owls had about the same food resources they had had in Siler's Bog. There were lagoons here, too, with frogs and salamanders and crayfishes that barred owls are fond of, and small snakes, lizards, mice, and gray squirrels in the drier parts of the woods. And they were even closer to Morgan Creek, in which barred owls sometimes waded to catch sunfishes and perch.

I was pleased to see the owls in Big Oak Woods. I could watch them more easily at the nest in the tall pine than in the hollow tree in the gloom of Siler's Bog, but I had one concern over their presence there. The previous

fall I had eartagged a cottontail rabbit in these woods and
had followed her movements that winter and spring.

With the barred owls hunting there, I could not be so sure
of the fate of the cottontail. There was, however, a good
chance that they might not catch her. The claws and feet
of barred owls are smaller and weaker than those of most
large owls, and they have been known to have difficulty
in attacking and killing a full-grown rabbit. So I had
reason to hope that Cottontail might survive during my
studies of her in the days ahead, especially if she could escape foxes and the more deadly horned owls and
red-tailed hawks of Laurel Hill.

CHAPTER IV
Cottontail

I saw the fourth week of March, windless and gentle, begin to crowd April. Starring the slopes of Laurel Hill and carpeting the floor of Big Oak Woods, pink-white spring beauties sent their warm fragrance across the drying Carolina fields. In a tuft of grasses, dead and brown, under a tall stalk of last year's horseweed, the pregnant cottontail rabbit crouched in her bed.

Last fall I had caught her in a box trap I had set in Big Oak Woods. While I held her warm body close, with one hand restraining her slashing, sharp-clawed hind feet, I had marked her with a small, harmless identifying tag that I attached to her right ear. She was only a few months old then and had already made the bed, or "form," in which she now sat, brown and still, twenty feet from the edge of the woods. It was one of several of her resting places I had found in which she might hide during the day. For a cottontail rabbit is a creature of dawn and dusk, and of the night. Watching her from the place where I stood on the old farm road, I could see the white tag in her right ear. Although I had seen other rabbits use her form briefly, the present occupant was Cottontail herself.

From my calculations, I knew that she would soon give birth to her second litter of the year. The first, born in February, had not done well. Barely hidden by the thin ground cover of late winter, crows had discovered it. From a distance I saw three of them at the nest, but I arrived too late to frighten them away. I suspected that two of them were the pair of crows that had nested for six successive years in a tall pine in nearby Finley Tract. The third may have been one of the pair that built a nest of sticks, lined with finely shredded bark and mosses, in a cedar tree a quarter of a mile away on Laurel Hill. While Cottontail ran at one crow, causing it to fly, the other two reached into the nest, and each flew off with a squealing young. By the next day, the three baby cottontails that were left had disappeared. The crows may have returned for them, or possibly Cottontail herself had moved them to another place.

From her bed in which she sat quietly on this March day, Cottontail could see straight ahead into leafless Big Oak Woods. And she could see even in back of her, through the spaces in the tuft of dead grasses that the winds had twisted around her three-pound body. Enemies come to a cottontail from all sides. Upward she could see the brown speck that hung two thousand feet away in the vast dome of blue above Laurel Hill. With her I watched the red-tailed hawk swing in circles, its head bent earthward, searching the North Carolina farm for the movement of any animal that might be suitable prey.

Cottontail tightened her body, as though preparing for a sudden leap and swift flight. Perhaps she was waiting for my sweeping glance to rest on her still form, but I ran my gaze over and beyond her, as swiftly as the running breeze that touched the grasses around her and then was gone. Had I looked too long, she would have known that I had discovered her and would have left her form in a swift dash across the field and into Big Oak Woods. She may have feared the red-tailed hawk more than she feared me. She kept her place.

Cottontail's large brown eyes—high in her head, just below the long, sensitive ears—gave her almost periscopic, or "around and around," vision. She could see, microscopically, the stink beetle that crawled up the grass past her moist, wobbling nose. Seconds later, she may have seen it snatched out of the air by a buzzing robber fly that sank its beak into the beetle and drained its life juices. I saw and marveled at the swiftness of the predatory fly's strike.

Cottontail's dark eyes remained fixed in a watchful stare. She may have seen the hurrying Tapinoma ant that ran from under her feet, but she gave no sign. A yard away, the ant tumbled into a conical pit made by an ant lion in the sand. Instantly the sicklelike jaws of the fiercely predatory insect reached up at the bottom of the pit to pull the ant under. Death by violence, even in miniature, was the cottontail's world. She herself might be struck down before she could bear the six young that had gradually swollen her double uterus these last twenty-seven days. At their places of attachment, the blood of her young now mingled with her own. Perhaps their stirrings warned her of the new venture for which she must now prepare. Within twenty-four hours, her litter would be born. One more task remained. . . .

෴ One of the miracles of the cottontail's world is its unusual breeding cycle. No wild mammal of North America, except some of the field mice, is more prolific. In the South, from February to July or August, the cottontail may have six or seven litters with an average of five young in each. In one summer, she can produce thirty-four young rabbits, and some of these may breed and have young before the long summer has ended. After five years, if Cottontail and all her progeny still lived, 3,779,136 rabbits would be swarming over the Mason Farm.

Of course, no such thing happens. The red-tailed hawks of Boothe Hill, the gray foxes of nearby Willow Oak Swamp, the bobcat of Edwards Mountain, the half-wild dogs, and the snakes, weasels, and hunters that move over the Mason Farm sweep most of them away. Only a remnant of the cottontail population lives through winter and into spring. These are the sustainers of the cottontail race. . . .

෴ The past winter I had seen the first of the wild "jump sequences" of the cottontail courtship that lead, in twenty-one days, to the first mating of the year. It began early in January in the dusk of a snowless field by Big Oak Woods near the place where I sat hidden in a tree. During the fall, Cottontail had abandoned her open-field bed for the security of a brush pile at the wood's edge. She was warmer there, protected from the north winds and touched for a few hours each day by winter sunlight. To be near Cottontail's winter bed, I had built a wooden platform above the ground. I had fastened it securely between the close-growing trunks of several trees and had wrapped it around with burlap. Hidden as in a wildlife photographer's blind, I could watch the brown field and the wood's edge below without being seen.

Late that mild January day, I heard a barred owl hoot from Willow Oak Swamp and saw a last cardinal flutter to its roost in a nearby cedar tree. Through an opening in the burlap, I saw Cottontail's brown shape leap from the brush pile. She moved out into the field, her white eartag showing in the dying light. This time she did not stop to groom her fur or to browse on sumac bark as she usually did on leaving her bed. Another cottontail had suddenly appeared, and I saw it follow her. From what I learned later, this was a male. He came toward her slowly from the rear. When he was ten feet away, Cottontail turned quietly to face him. She crouched and laid back her ears in the threat pose. She would accept his courtship up to a point, but that was all at this time.

The male, facing her five feet away, stood high on all fours, his ears straight up. Suddenly he rushed at her and Cottontail leaped high in the air. The action was so fast in the dusk that I could not see all, but while she is in the air, Cottontail is said to throw a jet of urine at the male as he passes under her. It is a part of the premating behavior that works both animals a little closer to the time of mating.

At the end of his rush the male turned, and both faced each other again. Now Cottontail dashed at him and he leaped over her, apparently throwing a jet of urine at her as he passed. Some of these jumps were tremendously long for such a small animal. In the winter snow I had measured the ordinary leaps of an undisturbed cottontail at from three to five feet and the wild bounds of a cottontail chased by a fox at from eight to nine feet; but some of these courtship jumps were twelve to fifteen feet long.

In the pale light of the gathering dusk, I saw the jump sequence suddenly end. The two brown forms moved away from each other and toward Big Oak Woods. There Cottontail began to nibble the bark from a young red maple along the wood's border; the male moved into the woodland and disappeared. Bark makes up most of the winter food of a wild rabbit, and not until April, with new grasses and fresh herbs, would Cottontail change gradually to the green foods of summer. . . .

🙢 My luck ran out that January in my observations of Cottontail's courtship sequences. I became seriously ill and for weeks was unable to hide in my blind and watch her. At the time, while I was recuperating from a severe respiratory infection, I worried over the fate of the small brown rabbit. However, I did not need to watch her to know what would follow, if she lived. Scientists had studied the breeding period of the cottontail rabbit so intensively that it had become one of the most thoroughly explored of any small wild animal.

Twice more in January Cottontail would join the male in the jump sequences. The jump periods would come at seven-day intervals, with Cottontail's increasing rhythmic urge, and that of the male, for close contact with each other. Each time the sequences would be longer and more fevered as the female approached her estrus, or "heat." The longer days of midwinter would bring more light; passing directly through a rabbit's eyes, or through its orbital tissues, the increasing light would stimulate the hypothalamus of Cottontail's brain, which in turn would cause her pituitary gland to give off increased sex hormones. This would start her breeding cycle.

In Cottontail the interaction of two ovarian hormones would bring cellular changes in her uterus and vagina and the ripening of her egg follicles. In the male it would lead to the forming of sperms in the testes.

If my calculations for Cottontail's courtship sequences that January had been correct, on the twenty-second day—seven days after the third and last jump sequence of the year—the male in the dusk would come after Cottontail, chasing her closely. One would barely be able to see them in the gathering gloom, but there would be no jump period at the time, for Cottontail would have reached her first heat, or estrous cycle, of the year. Thereafter, there would be no preparation by the jump sequences and her heat would come regularly every twenty-eight days until the spring and summer breeding season ended.

The male chasing Cottontail in the dusk would finally catch up with her. Cottontail, no longer resistant, would crouch in the submissive posture. He would mount her, and from that union probably would have come Cottontail's first unfortunate litter, which had been killed by crows.

Now in March, long after my illness and long after I had discovered that Cottontail was still alive, I was to see her complete her preparation for the birth of her second litter and to watch the surprising spectacle that immediately followed the birth of her young. . . .

ɚ For an hour I had been watching Cottontail crouched in her form. The mild March day was ending, and she would soon emerge from her bed to start her long night. I heard the sweet, piping cries of chorus frogs from the roadside ditch as I moved quietly toward my observation tree. A red-shouldered hawk began its musical wailing along Morgan Creek. Its cries must have startled the pileated woodpecker of Big Oak Woods. The big, red-crested bird cackled loudly and flew up to its roosting hole in the top of a giant oak. As I passed the frogs, they fell silent. Quietly as I had walked, they must have seen or heard me. By the time I had settled in my tree platform, their cries had started again.

At 6:00 p.m., Cottontail leaped out of her bed and sat for a moment in the low green grass. She reached down to lick her sides and, catlike, began to groom her fur. She sat up on her haunches and washed for forepaws with her tongue, then ran her paws down over her long ears. For a time she was busy with them, then she turned suddenly away and began to nibble at the March grasses and chickweed whose tender green was sweeping across the field.

Now Cottontail seemed nervous and she often stopped feeding to sit high on her haunches and look around. I saw that she was gradually moving to the center of the field. When almost at midfield, she stopped, sat up to look again, then dropped to all fours and began to dig with her front feet. She was digging her nest cavity, and I thought she had chosen the place wisely, or with inherited cottontail caution. Most of the foxes, raccoons, opossums, and other animals that hunt over the Mason Farm travel the farm roads or along the ditches, stream banks, and woodland trails. Out in the center of the old weedy field, a rabbit's nest with its young would be less likely to be discovered by hungry four-footed predators.

She did not dig long. Later, I discovered that she must have excavated most of the four-and-a-half-inch-deep cavity during the last few days because she now turned to the next operation to complete it. She ran away from the nest cavity to a clump of foxtail grass. Quickly she bit off the dried grasses and, with them crosswise in her mouth, returned to the cavity. I could see her put her head down and arrange the grass stems with her mouth and forefeet. Back and forth between grasses and her nest she traveled, stopping occasionally to browse the green stems of dandelion or to sit up and look cautiously around.

Suddenly, in the evening gloom of the March day, I saw another cottontail hop toward the nest. From what followed, I learned that this was the dominant male, perhaps the one that had sired Cottontail's first litter—and the second, for which she was now preparing. Behind him came four other rabbits that I could see were following Cottontail's tracks, their noses to the ground like trailing hounds.

Through my powerful binocular I watched the dominant male

vigorously chase them away, then return to the nest. He nosed over it carefully and was so preoccupied with it that when Cottontail returned, she had to hop around him to deliver another mouthful of dried grasses to her nest. He seemed to be inspecting her work, but he quickly left the nest to again drive away the four rabbits that had boldly returned to within a few feet of Cottontail. Obviously these were all her suitors, and the dominant male intended to keep them from her. But why were they all interested in a pregnant cottontail about to give birth to her young? Their behavior seemed curiously untimely, but I was soon to see the reason for it.

Very quickly Cottontail stopped carrying grasses to her nest and began pulling loose the molting hair from her shoulders and flanks. She had begun a new pattern of behavior. She had completed her grassy nest lining next to the raw earth. Now she was beginning the final inner nest lining of her own fur which would cradle her young and blanket them over from above. Their birth was imminent; her uterine contractions might even have begun.

As she pulled hair from her rump, I saw her fall. Her hind quarters seemed paralyzed as she sprawled helpless on the ground. She fell several times before she was able to stand again and go on with her hair pulling. Apparently the uterine convulsions that now periodically seized her caused her to lose temporary control over her hind legs.

While the male watched, Cottontail made several trips to the nest and worked the fur into the inner lining. She moved a little way from the nest and again began to pull at her fur. The male came close, smelled of her, then touched her with his forefeet.

Cottontail leaped on him and rode him to the ground. He squealed as she held him down by pressing one of her hind feet on his neck, and she bit him on the rump. He squealed again, and she released him and went back to her hair pulling. The other males drew closer and one of them ran around in impatient circles. The dominant male came close to her and smelled of her, but he did not touch her. Apparently he was checking something about Cottontail, but what it was mystified me.

Cottontail gave birth to her young quickly. I was watching her steadily through my binocular as she continued to pull at her fur while near the nest. Suddenly she stopped, turned, and squatted over the nest. Then she whirled about several times and ended up facing in the opposite direction. She straightened her back and jerked her pelvis downward. With this action I believe that she forcefully delivered one or more young into the nest chamber. Then she sprawled over the nest for about five minutes, looking straight ahead. From her position I think she nursed her newly born cottontails for the first time. The nursing over, she scratched dead grasses over the young, then dashed away.

I had suspected what was to come, but was not prepared for the strange behavior of the males that now began in the March dusk. Cottontail had moved to the edge of Big Oak Woods where the five attending males were waiting for her. She ran aggressively at them and drove them away, but when she turned from them, they followed her closely like hounds on a hot trail. All moved with ridiculous exaggeration, standing unusually high on their hind feet, deeply sniffing the air, and rapidly rotating their ears. They moved jerkily and often collided as they hopped wildly about.

Cottontail had slowed down, and the dominant male dashed at the others to keep them away. Then he turned and caught up with her. Now, instead of repelling him, she crouched submissively and he mounted. He made four swift pelvic thrusts and it was over. Cottontail broke away and moved into darkening Big Oak Woods. I saw her cottony white tail disappear in the darkness with the five males in pursuit.

With her loss of interest in the males, Cottontail would begin another behavior pattern in which she would closely guard her helpless young. She would remain somewhere not far from them, and to nurse them, for a day or two after they were born, she would crouch over the nest—belly down—with the young ones nuzzling her breasts from their hiding place in the nesting cavity in the ground. Each nursing time, before Cottontail left, she would rearrange the furry blanket and then scratch grasses over the nest to cover it.

Despite a rabbit's care in hiding her nest and young, dogs, foxes, skunks, cats, and large snakes find the helpless young ones and eat them. Sometimes shrews and field mice attack and kill the young in the nest. One day, along a logging road on Laurel Hill, I watched a weasel carry a young rabbit from a cottontail's nest and enter a pile of rocks in which the weasel had a family of its own. The rabbit's nest was empty and I suspected that the weasel had carried away every one of the cottontail young to feed them to her own litter.

One morning, in a grassy field above a pond, I saw a collie swallowing a young rabbit. Three dead ones, about ten days old, lay at the dog's feet. It had dug the young rabbits from the nest and had killed all of them just before I arrived.

ℰℰ A rabbit's devotion to its young can be pathetic when its efforts to protect them are futile. But it can be a splendid thing when a mother cottontail willingly confronts a relatively enormous foe to save her young from destruction.

One day a young North Carolina farmer told me a remarkable story of an adult rabbit, one that not only illustrated the animal's courage, but a kind of rabbit wisdom which required exquisite timing. It was an act of which I was sure Cottontail herself would have been capable. One spring morning, while he was plowing a field, the roar of his tractor frightened a rabbit from her hiding place in a patch of grass. When he walked to the place he found the rabbit's nest. It held four young ones about a week old, their eyes just opened. The farmer covered them again with the mother's protective blanket of grass and fur, drove a stick into the ground to mark the place, and continued his work. When he got to that part of the field, he plowed around the nest, leaving a small island of undisturbed land with the young rabbits in the center of it.

The next morning, when the farmer drove to the field to continue his plowing, he heard a sharp yelp in the distance. Then he saw a long-legged black dog and a smaller beagle gallop out of the woods and start across the plowed field. The stray dogs were roving aimlessly but with their noses to the ground and moving in the general direction of the rabbit's nest in the center of the field. The dogs were too far away for him to head them off. He shouted at them, but they came on, and within seconds would reach the cottontail's nest. Then, out of a blackberry patch at the field's edge flashed the brown form of an adult rabbit. Presumably it was the female cottontail that the young farmer had seen leave the nest the day before.

The rabbit crossed the field in tremendous bounds and reached the nest just ahead of the dogs. She ran to meet them, then swerved sharply and cut across the field in front of their noses. Surprised by the rabbit's boldness, the dogs stood like statues, their heads up, mouths open. Then with a roar they were after her.

The black dog was much swifter than the beagle. Within seconds he had overtaken the cottontail and was stretching, open-jawed, to catch her. Just as his mouth was closing on her rump, the rabbit jerked away in another direction. The black dog rushed past the cottontail, but the beagle changed direction with her and was very close to her bobbing white tail. Again the rabbit turned, but the black dog was there and about to seize her. She swerved once more and, with the dog's slavering jaws at her tail, dived into an open, grassy ditch that drained water from a nearby woodland across the field. The beagle plunged into the ditch after her.

The rabbit raced up the ditch bottom, a brown streak. The black dog, now running on the bank above the cottontail—his back arched, his long legs reaching far ahead—was closing rapidly. It seemed to the farmer that it was impossible for her to escape. He was sure then that the rabbit could not reach the woods ahead of the dogs. With the black one's muzzle almost touching her bobbing tail, the cottontail gained the edge of the road on which the farmer stood. But instead of trying to cross it as he had expected her to do, she suddenly disappeared. She had run inside a drainage pipe buried under the road.

The dogs, brought up short, howled and shoved their noses into the opening, but it was too small for them to enter. The rabbit, knowing her territory and all its escape routes and hiding places, had calculated her race to the last split second, and had won.

During the few hours of each March day that I tried to trace the survival of Cottontail and her growing litter, only once did I see her threatened by dogs, although the stray animals that ran about over the Mason Farm must have chased her many times. The miracle was that she, and her litter in the field, had survived at all, with the constant threat of death from so many natural enemies. But she proved to me that a cottontail might live for a relatively long time and that she has stratagems which protect her quite as effectively as her strong hind legs and her wisdom in keeping close to the woodland with its hollow logs into which a rabbit can escape if pursued too hotly by dogs, foxes, hawks, or owls. One March morning, Cottontail showed me a special ruse that I think she uses to outmaneuver an enemy when her litter is threatened.

At dawn I walked the east border of Big Oak Woods, hoping

that I might glimpse Cottontail before she had retired for the day to her bed. I had arrived at my tree-platform blind too late to watch for her in the early morning dark.

Suddenly, from the edge of the leafless woods ahead, I heard a loud bawling, then a chorus of frenzied yelps. Then I saw two tan-and-white dogs streaking westward under the leafless trees, hot on the trail of either a rabbit or a fox. From their starting point near the woods' edge, I was sure that they had frightened Cottontail from her bed under a brush pile, and when I arrived there I found that she was gone. I left the woods and stood on the road, listening.

The rabbit, if it were Cottontail, was doing a surprising thing. From the wild cries of the dogs, fading rapidly westward, it was apparent that she was leading them quickly and directly out of her territory. Usually a rabbit will run only a few hundred yards before circling and finally coming back almost to the bed from which the dogs started it. If, by that time, the rabbit's side jumps and backtracking have not shaken the dogs from its trail, it will usually turn away and circle in another direction, laying down another maze of scent trails to confuse the dogs, but staying inside its home area.

Within ten minutes I heard the hounds baying faintly from faraway Laurel Hill, just south of Muskrat Pond. Then they fell silent. I stood quietly for five minutes, then I heard one of the dogs howl long and dolefully. The animal's voice held a note of despair, and I knew that it had lost the trail.

I stood without moving for another ten minutes. There was no sound from the dogs and I heard only the lisping notes of a pair of Carolina chickadees in Big Oak Woods. Then came a light patter of feet, a mere whisper of sound from the woods. Some animal was coming toward me, but it was not a squirrel which moves with a rush of sound and a scattering of leaves on the forest floor. This sound was light as the drumming of first raindrops. It ceased, and I stood still, holding my breath. The sound came again, and suddenly, at the woods' edge I saw Cottontail. She leaped out on the road, stopped, and sat up. We were squarely in view of each other, not more than one hundred feet apart. Her brown body was twisted toward me, her ears high. I noted that her two front feet hung down over her narrow chest. I kept very still, scarcely breathing.

For a moment Cottontail held her pose. Apparently reassured, she dropped her front feet to the ground and leaped ahead into the grassy depths of the roadside ditch. She was hidden by the weeds and grass, but I heard her coming toward me. When opposite the place where I stood, she leaped out of the ditch to a grassy road that leads eastward across the open fields to Finley Tract Woods. Hopping slowly away, she did not travel far. When she reached a lone multiflora rosebush, she quietly disappeared under its protective, downcurving canes. There, as I discovered the next day, she had settled herself in another grassy bed in which I was to see her, off and on, all that spring. Her "form" under the rose bush was only a few hundred yards from her March litter in the old field, and I wondered if she might have chosen it to keep closer watch over her family. . . .

ළ When Cottontail's young were fourteen days old, they left the nest not to return. Each weighed about one quarter of a pound and began its first nibbling of green plant food in the April grasses and clover. Sometimes, in the day's-end gloom of the old field, I saw Cottontail sit up, I am sure, before a young one which had crept out of its grassy hiding place to nurse.

In three weeks the cottontails were weaned. As far as I know, some of them lived for a while within Cottontail's own four to six acres before they left to establish nearby territories of their own.

One April evening, I saw three of the young rabbits playing. They chased each other in small circles through the lengthening green grasses and over the dusty farm road. Early one morning, Cottontail herself joined one in a game in which the young one dashed at her and she leaped over its head. The small one turned and ran at her again, and Cottontail jumped high as it passed. Twice more they played their little game before it ended. The last that I saw of them, Cottontail's white tail was bobbing like a beacon ahead of the youngster as she led it under a thorny rose hedge.

The Winds
of April

March has wild winds, sharp with cold and the scent of old leaves; April has warm and fragrant winds that blow sweet across the Mason land. Out of the southwest the prevailing winds come, sweeping first through Laurel Hill Woods. On the upper slopes they strike the gray, still leafless trees, then shake the blossoms of shadbush and trillium, the purple dwarf iris, the wild ginger and nodding squirrel corn, the pink wood sorrel, the blue flowers of fawn's breath. Down, down, the slopes they go, stirring the brown leaves and picking up the sweetness of trailing arbutus, of hepatica and heartleaf, wood anemone, and the little windflower, wild cranesbill and blazing star, and the small, frail bluets.

At Muskrat Pond, they ruffle the surface in little gusts, blow up and over a bank of blue-eyed grass, and move eastward over the fields of purple henbit, starry chickweed, and wild toadflax. By the old farm roads and along the ditches, they sway the stems of lyre-leaved sage and touch the flowers of strawberry and yellow cinquefoil, half hidden in the grass. On and on they go, passing through the rose hedges and fluttering the husks of the old corn fields beyond, then restlessly onward into Willow Oak Swamp.

But the April winds have other uses than to bear the perfumes of the land and to attract the insects that pollinate the flowers. They are the carriers of the uncountable motes of golden pollen, shaken from the tall pines of Siler's Bog and from the male flowers—the catkins—of the oaks, hickories, and beeches of Laurel Hill and the alders, elms, willows, and birches along Morgan Creek.

Upward and outward the male pollen dust is blown, falling on the female flowers of these wind-pollinated trees, fertilizing them, and starting the first development of their seeds. The winds also are for insects to ride upon, carrying clouds of the gossamer-winged, frail creatures to far places, sometimes to three miles above the earth; for grasses and composites of the old fields to sail their winged seeds upon— to launch them, parachuted, in their aerial distribution across the land; and to speed the birds in their long migrations. And of all the birds that use the winds, some of the buteonine hawks know them best. The red-tailed and the red-shouldered seem born of them as they drift about in their courtships high in the April sky.

CHAPTER V

The Red-tailed Hawks of Boothe Hill

For five years I had followed the lives of the pair of red-tailed hawks that hunted daily over the Mason Farm. From the first it had been easy to tell the male from others of his kind. He was not only smaller than his mate, as the males of all hawks are, but he was darker brown than she and the other red-tailed hawks that sometimes soared over the North Carolina farm.

I knew the large female by her characteristic behavior and her individual markings that I had learned from three thousand hours spent in her woodland home. As one hill can shelter only one tiger, according to an Oriental proverb, so one tract of woods can support only one red-tailed hawk and her mate. I discovered that, occasionally, she permitted others of her kind to linger in the air over her home range, but adults exclusively, and only at certain times in midwinter and spring. Then she and the male allowed another pair that lived a mile to the east to join them in the wild exuberance of their nuptial flights.

These two—the small, dark male and his large, brown mate—may have held their home range over thousand-acre Laurel Hill for years before my coming. A pair of red-tailed hawks, together, are large enough and aggressive enough to drive out all others and to remain undisputed king and queen of their mile-square domain. Only one other kind of bird competes successfully with them for their nest, as I was to find out.

In three of those first four years I had known them, the redtails had used their old nest in a tall oak on Laurel Hill. In the fourth year, they moved about five hundred feet from the old nest and built a new one in a beech tree. That spring I discovered why. During the winter, before the wandering pair returned to the oak to claim their nest, a pair of great horned owls had taken possession of it. These large, fierce owls are probably the only birds in the North Carolina woods capable of challenging the red-tailed hawks for their rightful home.

The past year—the fifth one I had known the hawks—they had deserted their new nest for a reason known only to themselves. The owls still held the hawks' old nest, and for the first time since I had known them, the redtails disappeared from Laurel Hill. I knew that somewhere in the woodlands that covered the hills and valley slopes for five miles around they had another nest, for they continued to hunt over the Mason Farm. But though I searched for it through February and March, long before the green leaves covered the woods to make my search an almost impossible one, I never found it.

The female would have let me know, long before I came near,

78

that she had a nest. In her fearlessness and her determination to protect it, she would have flown to meet me. But in all my miles of hiking, her warning screams never came to me that spring. Now, in my sixth year with the hawks, I had seen the pair soaring over nearby Boothe Hill, an oak and hickory ridge that is an extension of Laurel Hill. Only Siler's Bog separates the two. This year I hoped to find the nest.

From his thousand-foot height over the Mason Farm, the male red-tailed hawk, in the blue April sky, could see forty miles in any direction. Watching him through my binocular, I could see him looking straight ahead and holding his place in the twenty-mile-an-hour wind. With slight aeronautic adjustments in the uptilt of his broad wings and small movements of his rusty-red tail, he remained fixed in the sky as though held there by a string. If he had looked southward he could have seen the bare brown fields and green pine woods receding mile after mile into heavily forested Chatham County; northwest, more rolling, pine-clad hills and fields stretching beyond Durham; and northeast, the smoky haze that marked Raleigh, the state capital, thirty miles away.

But the male redtail seemed to have no interest in the far distances. Now he was looking directly down at his mate, as she hung in the air three hundred feet below him. Beneath her, the bare corn-stubble fields of the Mason Farm were splashed red-purple with the flowers of henbit, and along Morgan Creek the dark blue of violets ran for a mile along its greening banks. At every field's edge of the old farm he might have seen the smoky-white patches of Johnny-jump-ups, and in Big Oak Woods the first green leafing of the hickories, sweet gums, and redbud trees.

Lying on my back, in a bed of bluets at the foot of Laurel Hill, I could comfortably watch the circling male redtail against an immense vault of blue. I held my binocular steadily to my eyes to watch his slightest movement. For a moment he had stopped circling. A lazy brown speck, he hung motionless as though suspended in time and sky.

Then he fell forward, like a diver leaving a cliff. With two quick beats of his wings, he shot downward at the female. The plunge came unexpectedly, with the dazzling speed of an earthbound rocket. The hawk's wings were drawn to his sides, and I heard the rush of air through his stiff flight feathers. His speed must have been more than one hundred miles an hour as his wild plunge carried him in seconds within striking distance of his mate. Just as he seemed about to collide with her, he spread his wings wide and shot up and over her. As he passed her, he reached down with his yellow feet, touched her lightly on the back, then bounded upward into the sky. With a shock of surprise at its suddenness, I realized that I was again watching their courtship flight.

The male had regained his previous height, and now he strayed away from his mate. He began climbing higher, turning in tight circles, his russet tail shining in the sun. The female was still circling lazily below him as he gained height. The male had reached at least fifteen hundred feet above the earth. Now he appeared a small brown spot against a giant white cloud that moved across the sky.

Again, with that amazing suddenness, he plunged toward his mate, the wind rushing past the wings drawn to his sides. This time, as he seemed about to strike her, she turned over and reached up to him. Their screams drifted down to me as the male, checking his speed, hung just above her, his talons reaching down to touch hers. For a moment their feet seemed to interlock and they tumbled over and over in the air. They separated, and the male again soared away in lazy circles. As they moved farther and farther apart, they seemed to have lost interest in each other. I knew then that the courtship flight was over.

ed I got up and moved into the woods. It was a long, steep climb up Laurel Hill, and when I gained the top of the ridge I would need to walk two miles southward over an old logging road. The woods on Laurel Hill were within the range of a large wild turkey which had become a legend among the local hunters. He was an old black gobbler that had lived on the Mason Farm for at least ten years. I had not only seen him, but had learned his story and what happened to this splendid bird. At the end of the woods road, I would descend into Siler's Bog and walk a mile through its greening thickets before coming to the bottom slope of Boothe Hill.

I knew, from finding the nests of this pair of red-tailed hawks in past years, that if the nest I hoped to find was a new one, the pair would have started it in late February or early March. Within a few days they usually complete most of the foundation of the thirty-inch-wide, two-foot-high nest, built of sticks eighteen inches long and half an inch in diameter. Then the hawks spend a few more days shaping the shallow inner nest depression and lining it with the bark of cedar and wild grape. About the middle of March, the female lays her two greenish-white eggs lightly spotted with brown, and begins her thirty-two days of incubation. By now, in April, I was sure that the young would have hatched or would be close to hatching. And from past experience I knew that the nest would probably be in the tallest tree on Boothe Hill, at a place somewhere not far from the woods' edge.

I followed Yancey Brook upward, against the downward flow of its slow-trickling waters. Its gradual descent of Laurel Hill, between banks of bluets and soft mosses, made an easier trail to walk than climbing directly up the steep, rocky slope.

I passed a deer trail that crossed the brook. It was a place where the pointed hooves of the animals had trodden deep into the moist banks. All during the past winter, the herd had traveled there. Each day, in the early morning and evening, they had crossed the brook, at this point halfway between their sleeping places in the pine thickets of Laurel Hill and their feeding grounds in the swamp below.

At winter's end, the herd had broken up. The bucks had retreated into the coolness of the swamp and now the tawny does were lying up on the sunny, wooded slopes, not far from the thickets in which they had hidden their recently born fawns. As I passed some young maples, I saw the freshly nipped branches that deer had browsed early that morning or during the night.

An April breeze starting up the slope brought me the delicate fragrance of flowering dogwood, spring beauties, and of trailing phlox. The canopy of trees overhead was still open, the tiny new leaves barely misting the tops with pale green.

I looked sharply into the upper branches of every tree. The red-tailed hawks might have nested somewhere on Laurel Hill this spring, and I might have missed seeing them despite my long winter's search. But I reached Siler's Bog without seeing a nest.

In the swamp I walked a mile under tall sweet gums and tulip trees round and straight as ships' masts. In the deepest part of the bog, I skirted dense greenbrier thickets and blackwater lagoons filled with piping frogs and brightened with patches of wild blue star and the whiteness of Atamasco-lilies. Then, just ahead, I saw the oaks and hickories that marked the beginning of the long slope up Boothe Hill. An hour later I was close to the top.

Suddenly I heard a wild scream—a long-drawn whistle that sounded like escaping steam. Then I saw the female red-tailed hawk flying low over the treetops. She was coming swiftly toward me. I was sure that her nest was not far away. Now the dark male, responding to his mate, came flying over the hill, soaring in from the Mason Farm and its fields and Big Oak Woods—his favorite hunting grounds. Both hawks were screaming and circling just above the trees.

I moved up the last part of the slope. One hundred yards ahead, at the place where it flattened, I saw a towering oak within a large grove and a mass of sticks in a crotch forty feet above the ground. It was the nest of the red-tailed hawks.

For observing the nest, the tree was in the best position of any I had ever found. The nest, in a crotch next to the trunk was on a level with the open top of the ridge and a pile of rocks in which I might hide. There were no leafy lower branches to interfere with my view of it from the ridge.

I climbed to the rocks. With the hawks screaming overhead, I looked down through my binocular and saw two downy white chicks lying flat in the nest. The young hawks were not more than a day old and were so weak that they could not stand. I thought I could see the small temporary tooth (on top of each fiercely hooked bill) with which, after hours of struggle, each chick cuts its way out of the egg.

The hawks were so young that I knew I must not keep the female away from the nest for too long. The newly hatched birds are extremely sensitive to chilling. If the mother does not brood them almost continuously during their first twenty-four hours, they may catch pneumonia and die.

As though to prompt me, the female dived with tremendous speed. As she came at me, I heard the wind rushing past her folded wings and saw her dark eyes blazing into mine. I felt my skin prickle and a chill of fear ran over me. Although large hawks have dived at me near their nests many times, I have never gotten used to the dazzling speed at which they approach and the intimidation of the flashing eyes, the forward-thrust feet—with their curved talons—and the formidably hooked bill.

Instinctively I ducked, crouching low among the rocks. I felt a rush of air from the hawk's five-foot spread of wings, and when I looked up, she had turned away from just over my head and was flapping upward in a wide circle, preparing for another dive. I have never had a red-tailed hawk strike me in defense of its nest, but one of these anxious birds might do so.

Now the male sped down upon me, filling the air with his screams as he came, but he, too, ended his dive above my head. I felt the stir of air from his wings as he swept by and flapped upward in a steep climb. Both hawks were screaming with rage and seemed determined to drive me quickly away.

I climbed down from the rocks and walked swiftly toward the grove. As soon as I reached the sheltering trees and started down the wooded slope, the hawks stopped their diving but continued to scream and to circle just over the treetops.

I had left the nest area rapidly, but not before I had noted another feature that would favor my observation of the nest. A deep ravine led upward from the far side of Boothe Hill to the pile of rocks. It was densely overgrown with wild rhododendron thickets which would screen my approach. By following the ravine I might reach the ridge without alarming the hawks, even if one of them was on the nest. . . .

Within two days I had built a roofed canvas blind among the rocks. From peepholes in its sides I could watch the nest without being seen by the hawks. Although the birds screamed and dived at me while I worked on the blind, the small structure did not seem to bother them after it was in place.

Day after day, while hidden in the blind, I watched the male bring food to the female, which she fed to the young. In the beginning, he brought small animals—mice and cotton rats— which the female tore into tiny bits of bone and flesh. Then she held her beak down to the chicks, which instinctively picked at the smallest pieces adhering to her bill.

I was impressed with the big female's gentleness, and as she walked about in the nest, I noticed that she took great care not to step on her helpless young. But despite her concentration on them, she never lost her alertness and she was keenly aware of all that went on in the forest about her. Often I saw her lift her head and stand tense and watchful at some sound in the woods too faint for my ears. I think her hearing was relatively as keen as her magnificent eyesight.

Once, when her back was to me, I shifted in my hiding place. At the slight sound, the hawk swiveled her brown head sharply in my direction, her red-brown eyes staring fiercely from under her craggy brows. I seemed to feel her gaze burning through the canvas sides of my blind, but she finally turned away to stare moodily through the greening woods.

During the middle of the day, she spread her wings, tentlike, to shelter her young from the heat of the sun; when it was raining, she sat over them like a broody hen; at night she slept on the nest to protect them from chilling. I saw the male only when he came to the nest with food, and I assumed that he spent the nights roosting in some tree not far away.

While the young ones were very small, during the first week of their lives, the male fed the female while she remained on the nest. If she left, it was only briefly: to catch deer mice of the forest floor close by or moles that occasionally came out of their earthen tunnels to hunt over the ground for beetles and the grublike young of bumblebees in nests under stumps and leaves. And so the hunter was often the hunted in the woods of Boothe Hill.

Sometimes, when the female redtail returned, instead of carrying food in her beak she held a sprig of pine which she tucked into the nest beside the young hawks. I was to discover that this was not only decorative but functional. Later, when the young hawks grew larger and their appetites were fiercer—and the female had to leave them for long periods to hunt—I saw them hide under the green sprays of pine to escape the heat of the midday sun.

Once, during a brief absence by the female, I saw one of the young hawks back to the edge of the nest to excrete. It went too far, slipped over the edge and clung there, beating its small wings desperately. It was still trying to climb back when the female returned. As she alighted on the rim of the nest, she did not try to help the young bird but fed the one in the center of the nest. Apparently, she did not recognize the young hawk's plight and her instinct to feed the one within the nest was so strong that she ignored the one on the outside. Fortunately the youngster climbed back, at which the female turned to it and offered it the remainder of a mole she had fed in part to the other.

This explained to me why at least one of a brood of very young red-tailed hawks is often discovered dead at the base of the nest tree or disappears from the nest and is never found. Up to three weeks of age, they are clumsy and easily fall if they get too near the edge or are pushed by a scrambling nest mate. The more young hawks there are in the nest—sometimes there may be three or even four—the more likely it is that one may be crowded out and fall to the ground. The numbers of all animals are adjusted to their world, in part, by death of some of the young. These are the expendable. Apparently the fallen nestling, even if it is not killed, is never recovered by the parent birds. During the night it may become a meal for a raccoon or an opossum. And what the raccoon or opossum fails to eat, the shrews and the ants will carry away.

When the hawks were a little more than three weeks old and still covered with the white down of babyhood, they no longer crouched in the nest but were able to stand. From my blind I saw them walking around in the nest. They were now keenly aware of their world and cocked their heads to watch a yellow jacket buzzing around meat scraps left in the nest. When the wasp bit off a piece of meat and flew away, like the hawks, it, too, was carrying food to feed its own hungry young—small white grubs whose heads protruded from each cell of a paper nest underground.

After the wasp left, the young hawks bobbed their heads and focused their keen eyes on a pair of yellow-throated warblers that fluttered about in the green leaves overhead. The warblers were picking tiny caterpillars from the oak leaves and carrying them to

their young in a nest
at the tip of a branch not ten
feet above the hawks' heads.

The adult red-tailed hawk does
not try to catch such small birds. They
are too agile for it. Besides, the warblers are
usually too small to make their capture worthwhile
for a large bird of prey. The warblers, seeming
to know this, nested within thirty feet of the hawks.
And because no bird-eating Accipiter, such as the small,
sharp-shinned hawk, would dare to come near
the nest of the redtails, the warblers
gained protection from their
large companions.

ঌ I saw only a single incident in which one of the adult hawks tried to catch a bird. Early one morning I had crawled into the blind at daybreak. The faint gray light had streaked through the woods just sufficient for me to see the nest. Neither adult hawk was in sight, and I assumed they had spent the night roosting in a tree nearby.

The sun was filtering its first, long rays through the woods when I heard a light clucking sound. A hen turkey, followed by five half-grown young ones, stepped out from behind an arrow-wood thicket. They started across the woodland clearing near the nest-tree. Then, from nowhere, the female redtail suddenly swooped down at the wild turkey chicks, and in that instant, the ten-pound hen rose into the air to meet the three-pound hawk. With every dark feather swollen and her eyes blazing, the turkey closed with the redtail. But the redtail had had enough even before the turkey's powerful wings and big feet struck at her. The hawk, without checking her flight, veered sharply away and shot straight up to alight in a nearby oak. The young turkeys had disappeared into the safety of the Boothe Hill thickets, and the hen, still clucking, turned to follow them. The redtail sat for a few moments preening her disordered feathers. Then she turned and flew silently away through the forest.

ঌ At five weeks the white down on the backs and wings of the young hawks had been replaced by brown, mottled feathers, but their heads and flanks were still downy white. Now they often flapped their wings and danced about, leaping a foot or more into the air. When their feet struck the nest again, they grasped playfully at sticks or tugged at them with their beaks. They were strengthening their wings and neck muscles and the grip of their talons for the serious business of hunting and killing their own prey in the months ahead.

One day I saw the larger one flap its wings and run far out on the large branch that supported the nest. I knew then that the time for the young hawks to leave the nest permanently was approaching—perhaps in another week or ten days. Both young hawks were now so powerful and their appetites so ferocious that when one of the adult birds returned to the nest with a cottontail rabbit or a gray squirrel, the young ones swarmed over it and tore it greedily from the adult's grasp.

At six and one half weeks the larger of the young hawks, completely feathered, had left the nest. It returned from perching in a nearby tree only to use the nest as a feeding platform when an adult brought in prey. Now the food was no longer moles and mice, but mostly cottontail rabbits, gray squirrels, and once, a muskrat that one of the hawks had probably killed along Morgan Creek. I had sometimes seen muskrats boldly foraging during the day on the stream banks and had suspected they would make easy prey for a hawk or a fox.

On June 3, forty-nine days after hatching and a few days after its larger companion had gone, the remaining young hawk, which I assumed from his smaller size was a male, left the nest not to return. I saw him go quietly, as one leaves a room without shutting the door, and without looking back. He leaped into the air, flapped twice, then glided straightaway through the forest. When I returned to my blind the next morning, the young hawks were not in sight. But I heard them screaming in Siler's Bog at the foot of Boothe Hill and knew they were following the adults about or impatiently waiting in some tall tree to be fed.

ⱸ All through June and July the young hawks harassed their parents for food. Each day, while I walked over the five miles of farm road on the Mason Farm, I saw the young hawks or heard them screaming in the distance: *Pur-lee! pur-lee! pur-lee!*

In late June, I watched their first clumsy attempts at hunting. One morning, at daybreak, I saw one of the young hawks on the ground at the edge of Big Oak Woods. It was trying to catch a grasshopper and ran and leaped about, chasing it with wings held high. When I walked toward the young hawk, it flew, followed by the other, which had been perched in a tree, hidden in the woods.

The tameness of these young hawks during their first few weeks out of the nest was extraordinary. One day I stood on the farm road not four hundred feet from them while they tried to pounce on mice in the grass of an old field. But so fruitless were their efforts that I am sure they would have starved had not the adult hawks hunted food for them.

One hot July day, I saw one of the adults flying slowly along the border of Laurel Hill Woods with a small cottontail rabbit dangling from its talons. Both young hawks flew after it screaming loudly. Over an open field the adult dropped the rabbit. The larger of the two young hawks, in close pursuit, swooped down and snatched up the rabbit just as it hit the ground. Without checking its speed, it flew on, followed by the second young hawk. Both disappeared in the woods, still screaming.

Later I saw an adult drop a mouse to one of the young hawks, which grabbed it out of the air in its talons, then flew with it to the branch of a tall tree at the edge of the woods.

By August the young hawks had begun to catch mice and young rabbits on their own, but they made mistakes from which I think they learned. Late one afternoon I saw one of them soar from its tree perch at the edge of Finley Tract. In a long glide it descended to the far edge of a field and pounced on something in the grass. For a moment the hawk bounced up and down as though in the grip of its intended prey. Through my binocular I could see that it had seized a large cottontail rabbit, but so vigorously did the animal kick and leap about that the surprised bird released it and flew away. Apparently, the hawk had not grasped the rabbit properly and the cottontail had buffeted it severely.

On another August day, I saw the larger of the young hawks—presumably the female—make a dangerous mistake. I was walking southward over the old farm road past a rose hedge when I saw the young hawk gliding lower and lower over a grassy field. She was turning and twisting in flight, as though following some animal that was moving through the grass. Suddenly she dived out of sight and I heard a yowl of rage. Immediately the hawk appeared above the grass. Beating her wings powerfully, she flew straight up into the air. As she rose, several of her feathers floated away. Then a black cat raced out of the field, crossed the road, and disappeared into Big Oak Woods.

The hawk flew rapidly toward Laurel Hill and alighted in a tree at the woods' edge. Through my binocular I saw her shake out her ruffled feathers and begin to preen them. Occasionally she looked back at the place where she had tried to seize the cat. She seemed frightened by the experience, and I doubted that she would ever make such a mistake again. The cat might have disabled her, or might even have killed her.

ed By September, I no longer heard the young hawks screaming or saw them on the Mason Farm. As soon as they had learned to hunt they had either drifted away to new hunting grounds or had been driven off by the parent birds. After the nesting season is over, there is no room on the permanent range for other than the adults themselves.

One golden October day I climbed Boothe Hill to look again at the nest of the hawks, perhaps to assure myself that it was still there. It was flattened from its long summer of use, and the sticks that composed it were dry and dusty in the autumn sun. But near the center of it I saw a fresh sprig of green pine. Not long ago, perhaps that very day, one of the hawks had put it there. It was a sign of their continuing interest in the nest, their badge of ownership to their home in the oak. It was also clearly a promise—perhaps a slender one in a world where man with his gun and his misunderstanding is still the greatest threat to this bird that loves the freedom of the skies. But the promise was there. I saw it in the pine, and in its green hope for the hawks and for another spring.

*Water
for a
Cotton Gin*

꿱 Once there was a pond in Morgan Creek. It was only a little way south of the elm-shaded lawn where the old Mason Plantation house stood on what is now Finley Golf Course. The Reverend Mason created the pond when he built a dam to back up the creek waters for power to turn the wheels of his cotton gin.

The pond lay there, one hundred years ago, deep blue under summer skies but blue-white with ice and snow in winters that were colder than they are now. In April, the little hyla frogs must have piped from its shores, telling the Mason girls that spring and the wildflowers had come. Within another month, the frog chorus was in full cry and the first fireflies rising from the grass in the warm dusk. By day, glittering-winged dragonflies darted about in the sun over the waters, and pink Sabatia, yellow primrose, and the frail white Erigeron flowered on the pond's banks.

The Reverend Mason must have noted these signs and flags of spring and summer, for he wrote about the first June katydids he heard each year and the first eggs he found of the nesting "partridge." Sometimes he wrote of the pond in his diary . . .

January 3, 1879 . . . A very cold day. Students skating on the pond. Mercury at 20 before sundown. . . . January 12 . . . the largest freshet today in Morgan's Creek that has been for a great while. My dam broke. . . . January 14 . . . I worked on the broken dam. John Watson hauled ice from

the pond today. . . . February 3, 1880 . . . Pond full of
water. Went to ginning cotton. . . . March 9 . . . A heavy
rain last night, a flood of water at the gin. Something caught
in the wheel, I cannot gin until the water falls and
I can get it out. . . .

There is no record of when the old pond disappeared, but
after the Reverend Mason died, the dam on Morgan Creek
must have fallen into disrepair. Then, one day, on the tide of
a summer flood, it must have gone out, washed downstream
with all its frogs and fishes, its dragonfly and damsel fly
nymphs, and the host of small life that loves the still waters.

Long, long afterward, a new pond came to the Mason Farm,
built not on Morgan Creek but south of it, in an old field at
the foot of Laurel Hill. It was a pond built by the University
of North Carolina in 1965, for the use of its students in their
studies of the water's millions of living things. It was the
pond to which I came, in all its raw newness, to watch, to
listen, and to discover.

CHAPTER VI

The Tenants of Muskrat Pond

In the blackness of the warm May night, I drifted silently in my boat on the Mason Farm pond. I heard the sharp clicking calls of the tiny cricket frogs at the water's edge, the soft trill of tree frogs, and the strange little screams of Fowler's toads that also had come from the woods to seek their mates at the pond's edge. Above the bedlam of smaller frogs and toads, I heard the rumbling bass of big bullfrogs hidden in the pondweeds on the surface of the water, their stuttering moans sounding like the calls of animals in mortal distress. At times the amphibian chorus was so loud that I could not have heard a fox bark or an owl hoot had one called one hundred feet away in the edge of Laurel Hill Woods. Yet, only ten months before, there had been no frogs here, only the raw basin of a newly dug pond.

I switched on my light to single out each frog by its glistening, puffed-out throat bubble and saw the individual pairs of their eyes shining in the dark.

During one of the lulls in the frog chorus I had turned off my light and was sitting quietly, when I heard a soft splash. It came from the south end of the pond. I switched the flash on again and shot the beam across the water. In the brightly illuminated spot I saw a small brown form reared on its hind legs in the shallows. It was a muskrat, and it was gripping with its forepaws the upright stem of a cattail stalk.

In the brief moment that I saw the animal in the glare of the light, it seemed to be gnawing at the cattail as a beaver might gnaw at a tree. But this was not a beaver. Although its fur, like a beaver's, was rich brown and glossy, I could see that the animal was smaller. Besides, I knew muskrats on sight, having trapped them when I was a boy. This one weighed about three pounds— they weigh from one and a half to four pounds—and it was about twenty inches long from the tip of its moist black nose to the end of its naked tail. The nine-inch tail, had I any doubt of what the animal was, identified it for me: a black, slender, thinner-than-high tail; not the wide, flat, boardlike tail of a beaver.

I saw it holding its tail straight back, propping its body with the tail while it worked. After turning to look at my light, it dived with a splash into deeper water and was gone. This was one of the few times I had surprised a muskrat at night, although I have seen them by day. They are nocturnal and are especially alert in the dark outside of their burrows. One must sit quietly for long hours to see them either by night or by day. Once I saw one in the bright glare of noon in a field far from water, but that was before the pond had been built. It was in late summer when the crisis of a terrible drought was upon them and muskrats had left the dried stream bed of Morgan Creek to seek the safety of water and their plant food elsewhere.

I don't know the exact March day the muskrats arrived. But when I saw them there in the first spring of the pond's life, they gave me a name for the unnamed gem of blue waters that lay at the foot of green-clad Laurel Hill.

Surrounded on the south and west by woods of pine and oak, on the north by gurgling Morgan Creek, and on the east by the open fields of the old farm, Muskrat Pond attracted animals from miles around. All were drawn there because of the animals and plants that had come to live in its waters or along its shores. Some came to prey upon the animals of the pond, others were there to stalk those that came to hunt. In time, even the muskrats were in danger, though they were high in the scale of living things, far above their microscopic companions that swarmed in waters millions of times richer in life than any comparable area on land.

Among the outsiders, the birds came first—herons, wild ducks, and a lone osprey that soared about for a little while high over the waters, then left because there were no fishes in the new pond. Late in the pond's first winter, from the trails I saw along the banks, I knew that raccoons and gray foxes had found it, and when the waters grew less muddy, the deer came there to drink.

In the previous summer, the University of North Carolina officials had approved the building of the pond for the field studies of its Botany Department. Earth movers and trucks arrived, and in only a little while a low field in the northwestern corner of the Mason Farm had been dug deeper and the excavated earth piled in a ten-foot-high dam at the north end, not far from Morgan Creek. And it was from Morgan Creek that the pioneering muskrats came, deserting some of their old burrows in the creek banks to dig new ones in the raw banks of the five-acre pond.

I first saw muskrats there on a night in March when the feverish unrest of the mating season was on them, a time when they leave the security of their old burrows and move about in search of mates and new homes. In the faint light of the stars and the new moon low in the west, I saw two small, dark heads moving across the black waters, and the silver ripple that marked each watery trail. Perhaps this was a mated pair—I do not know. But from the series of freshly dug burrows I saw later in the wide, high dam, I am sure they were the first muskrats to arrive. And with what I knew from years of studying these animals in many places, and in following their trails about Muskrat Pond, I was able to put together the stories of their lives.

ও During the pond's first autumn and winter, while the earthen basin was filling with water, microscopic life appeared there. And it was upon this almost invisible life that all life in the pond was to depend, including the muskrats themselves. It came in the waters of the brook called Buckhorn Branch that trickles down Laurel Hill and feeds a six-foot canal at the pond's southern end. It came in the silver rain of autumn that overflowed the springs in the woods above; it came with seeds and spores wafted there by the winds; it may have washed there with the melting snows high on Laurel Hill. Perhaps, most of all, it had come to Muskrat Pond on the trailing feet of wild ducks that paddled the waters of other ponds and carried there the beginning algae and small green plants. These, with the radiation of the life-giving sun, would oxygenate the new waters and build a chain of animal life so vast as to stagger one with its multiplicity of numbers and kinds.

In the dark waters through which the muskrats swam, their brown furry bodies moved past billions of tiny green and yellow plants so small that only a microscope can reveal their strange forms; past microscopic animals neither walking, creeping, nor swimming, but simply floating in such enormous numbers that they are called—by far—the most numerous animals on earth. This is the green, blue, brown, and gray world of plankton that gives not only colors to waters, but life to every creature from diving beetles and dragonflies to fishes, frogs, and snapping turtles. For the microscopic plant and animal plankton is the basis of all life in a pond—the pastures of the world of water.

The smallest grazers were there in millions—tiny rotifers, copepods, ostracods, and cladocerans. And there were also aquatic worms, snails, tadpoles, and small water insects (midge larvae and mayfly nymphs) that also ate the tiny plants. I had seen these smaller animals attacked and eaten by large insects—by giant water bugs, water-scorpions, and the nymphs of dragonflies and damselflies. Fishes, frogs, and turtles ate them, and I had seen these, in turn, attack and eat each other. I had spent long hours looking deep into these new waters, involved in the battle of the underwater community to survive. Even when I had seen no visible life there, I had felt the pull of the pond in a mesmeric experience comparable to that of looking into an open fire. We came from water, and it was there that the primitive cells began before we came ashore. Before the human hand was a hand, it was foreshadowed by the scaly foot of the snapping turtle, the furry paw of the muskrat.

ɘᶾ But the muskrats knew nothing of the plankton and its associated life in the waters through which they swam. They do not feed on plankton directly. Their hunger is for the rooted plants in the shallows. In March, their mating had been accomplished and their burrows dug. The nest chamber at the end of the main burrow in the dam had been lined with cattails that had sprung from windblown seeds in the shallow waters during that first spring of the pond's life. The muskrats knew when these sprouted; perhaps they smelled the tall, green, swordlike leaves of those first few plants. The morning after that May night when I had seen the muskrat cutting his cattails, I saw the partly eaten green stalks lying on the quiet waters. He had cut them down as a lumberjack might fell a tree.

ɘᶾ When the muskrats invaded the new pond in early spring, it was the female that dug the first burrows in the high dam. With the urgency of a home for her unborn young upon her, she had dug them with the skill of an engineer. I saw the opening to the first, or main burrow, one several feet out from shore and under about three feet of water.

One night, using only her forepaws and scratching like a dog, she started the burrow underwater, heading in the direction of the dam. Perhaps her instinct told her to start the opening far enough

below the surface that
it would not be
exposed by the
evaporative
losses of water
in summer. Un-
less a drought
came, the opening
would be under-
water at all times,
giving the muskrat and her

youngsters safe passage between the den and the pond.

Her sharp claws must have made good progress, for during the first night she dug her six-inch-wide by eight-inch-high burrow several feet toward the dam. As she worked, the muskrat scraped the earth backward on the pond bottom. Water filled the hole and immersed her as she dug, but she surfaced frequently to gulp fresh air for a few seconds, then plunged below again to renew her digging. Sometimes she stayed under for twelve minutes, but the more vigorously she worked, the more often she came up for air. I knew from handling muskrats I had trapped as a boy that she had an adaptation for cutting roots and other obstacles underwater without drowning: she can close her split lips tightly behind her four incisor, or biting, teeth, thus sealing out the water while she works. As she dug she slanted the burrow upward at an angle of about forty degrees. This would carry her tunnel well back into the dam above water line and yet keep it below the surface of the ground.

After two nights, she had dug into the dam well above the water level of Muskrat Pond. Still slanting her burrow upward, she stopped during the third night, when she bit into the deep roots of the soil-holding lespedeza plants that grow on the top of the dam. Touching them warned her that she was near the surface of the ground. There she ended her burrow and dug a den about two feet long, eight inches wide, and nine inches high. Then she lined it with soft rushes, grasses, and cattail stalks that she gathered from the south end of Muskrat Pond. It might have been "she" and not "he" that I saw in the beam of my light cutting a cattail that night in May, because one cannot tell the sexes of muskrats unless one examines them closely. Males and females are identical except that the females have three to five pairs of nipples on the belly between the front and hind legs.

Muskrats can and do breed in any month of the year, but in parts of the South they may begin in late winter and end their breeding in September. The female may have from one to five litters a year, but two or three is more usual. There are three peaks in the mating: the last of March, the last of April, and the last of May. The female bears from one to eleven young, but her average litter is from four to seven. She is pregnant from twenty-two to thirty days; the average pregnancy is twenty-eight days.

I guessed that the female which dug her main burrow in the dam of Muskrat Pond must have had at least three litters the first spring and summer of the pond's life. After she had completed her main burrow, she dug four others between the dam and the pond, with interconnecting tunnels for quick escape if a mink surprised her or her young in the den. I had seen the tracks of a large mink along the pond's edge, and I had wondered how long it might be before it confronted the muskrats. A mink is a professional killer, according to my old-time trapping friends—that is, it kills to stay alive just as any hawk, owl, bobcat, fox, or other carnivore will. And a mink can be fond of the flesh of muskrats, especially young ones; although I knew of some tough old muskrats that had stood off the attacks of minks and had even chased them out of muskrat burrows.

But the young muskrats may know many ways of dying before fate can put them in the path of a mink. The mother, frightened from her nest by a man or a mink, may rush down her burrow and into the water, unintentionally dragging her blind, almost-hairless newborn young that cling tightly to her nipples while nursing. Each is about four inches long and weighs only three fourths of an ounce. Some of them drop from the mother's breasts when she strikes the water and drown before she can retrieve them.

When the muskrats are about two weeks old, their eyes open. Their fur is gray, soft, and wooly, and each weighs from two to four ounces. Now they leave the nest for the first time and wander down the burrow to the waters of the pond. There they begin to swim and dive and climb on floating objects. But if this is playtime for them, it is also a dangerous time. Not only hawks and owls and foxes stalk them, but they may be attacked by a fungus disease which at this age is fatal to them.

At three to four weeks they are eleven inches long from nose to tail tip and have stopped nursing. Now they wander into the pond to eat tender grasses and other plants. They can swim and dive well, and some of them have become brown-furred like the adults; others will remain gray until autumn. If they see a hovering hawk, to escape its swift plunge they can submerge for up to three minutes or hide among marsh plants at the water's edge. But when they try to return to the nest they may find that their mother will turn savagely on them. She has had another litter, and not only will she threaten the weaned ones but if they do not leave she may kill them: sensing their hunger for protein, she knows they may turn cannibal and eat her newly born young.

Stress among too many muskrats living close together can cause terrible fighting, during which many of the wandering young are killed by their elders or fatally slashed by irritable ones their own age.

Mites, fleas, roundworms, flukes, tapeworms, and other parasites may weaken the young muskrats so much that they become easy victims of predatory animals; they suffer from abscesses, septicemia, coccidiosis, leukemia, and gallstones. Some of their diseases become epidemic and wipe out entire populations of both young and old.

I first saw young muskrats in the pond on a day in June. The mists were rising from the water and the yellow light of the morning sun lay soft on the woods of Laurel Hill. I was not expecting to see muskrats, but much of the excitement of my walks to the pond had come from the unexpected. A burst of music, wild and lyrical, gushed from an orchard oriole at the woods' edge. It was as though the bird had discovered some sudden secret joy; then it fell silent.

Muskrat Pond lies partly in a protective arm of wooded Laurel Hill. From the place where I sat on the grassy strip that encircles the pond, I looked south to the wooded cove and the green curve of trees reflected in the water. Brightening the tall grass all around the pond's edge grew patches of summer wildflowers: yellow sundrops and ragwort, white daisies and Queen Anne's lace, purple wood sorrel, and frost-blue skullcap. The sweet smell of fresh water mingled with the fragrance of the wildflowers.

In the shallows along the south shore, I saw islandlike thickets of tall green cattails—the muskrat's basic food—and the green stems of rushes and low-growing water purslane. And it was up these plant stems, under the protection of night, that I had seen soft-bodied dragonfly nymphs crawl from the water to the miracle of their transfiguration. In the beam of my light, I had watched the skin of these small clinging brown gnomes split down the back and fairylike creatures with glittering wings and bodies of flashing green and blue emerge. In the morning, when the warmth of the sun had dried the wings and bodies of the adult dragonflies, I saw them fly from the plant stems in their first flights. With fierce hunger, and like tiny hawking war-planes, they darted low over the water, sweeping their food of midges and mosquitoes out of the air.

Throughout that first year of the pond's life I had watched its changing face: the autumn glory of its reflected red and gold; the somberness of winter's purple and black; the hundred-shaded greens of soft-hued spring; the darkness of storms; and the blue vault of sky with white clouds sailing. At night, as the earth turned, I saw on its surface the glitter of stars moving down the sky and the silver moon's path. There were days when the brilliance of the sun on water was blinding; others when a wall of gray rain almost hid Laurel Hill and pockmarked the pond with little craters and splashing drops of silver. On some mornings the blue mists drew a veil across the pond's face, but always Laurel Hill brooded in the background. Even on the darkest nights I saw its curving line silhouetted blackly over the western half of the pond waters.

eð I turned away from the south shore and glanced northward to the dam. Suddenly I saw an enormous raft of whirligig beetles, fifty feet long and ten feet wide. The closely packed beetles moved slowly across the dark waters, sending little riffles ahead as the leaders pushed across the surface. There were at least two hundred thousand of them, and I realized with a quick thrill that never before had I seen so many together.

eð The blue-black whirligigs are the only beetles that live on the surface film of the water. They shoot swiftly ahead, whirl about in giddy circles, or dive below the surface in their search for insects living or dead. I have often watched them pop up from below to renew their oxygen supply by capturing a bubble of air between the tips of their wings and their bodies. Then they quickly dive again to continue their hunting underwater. Besides their ability to carry their air supply and to breathe below the surface, whirligigs have remarkable eyes. One pair is on top of the head, with which to see above the surface; another pair on the underside enables them to see below it.

A rattling call across the pond aroused me from my absorption with the whirligig beetles. I saw a blue-and-white kingfisher alight in a dead pine at the border of Laurel Hill Woods. It gazed sharply at the water, then dived from the tree into the shallows. When it struggled out of the pond, it held a bullfrog tadpole in its bill. It flew back to the pine and alighted on a dead branch. I saw a flash of the tadpole's white belly as the bird swallowed it. It was one of some one hundred thousand bullfrog tadpoles that I had estimated were swimming about like small fishes in Muskrat Pond that morning. They had wintered in the leaves at the bottom of the deep canal at the south end of the pond.

With the first warm days of March and April the tadpoles had spread through the shallows to rasp with their mouths at the algae on the underwater stems of cattails and pondweeds. Next year, or the year following, the bullfrog tadpoles—the only ones in the pond requiring more than a year to become adults—would lose their fishlike tails and become bullfrogs. Bullfrogs are meat eaters and fiercely predatory on dragonflies and their nymphs, other frogs, and tadpoles which might even be of their own kind. Some of them might also leap into the air to catch small birds and bats that sometimes skim low over the pond and its banks.

I was to see the hundred thousand tadpoles largely melted away; first by the deadly "redleg," a bacillus disease that swept through them and left hundreds of floating dead, and then by the raccoons and minks, and the herons, mergansers, and grebes that came to feed on the living tadpoles in the shallow waters. But the dead were not allowed to foul the pond for long. Crayfishes at night, and planarian worms moving near the shores, fed upon them, and the waters became clean again.

❧ With the suddenness of all unexpected things, the young muskrats appeared. I was looking below the pond's surface near the dam, when I saw the bottom suddenly clouded with mud at the burrow openings. Six young muskrats torpedoed from the tunnels and moved swiftly along the bottom of the pond. In the clear waters they appeared grayish with silvery undersides. They moved swiftly, striking out with their partly webbed hind feet in alternate strokes, and wriggling their snakelike tails to help them make quick turns as they darted about.

I could see that they did not use their small forepaws in swimming but held them, palms in, close up under the chin. Four of them turned back into the main burrow, but two swam farther out and disappeared in the dense beds of Chara, an algae which in the first months of the pond's life had spread thickly over the bottom.

I was watching for the reappearance of the two on the far side of the pond. Suddenly they broke the surface and swam quietly ashore. I saw them climb out on the low bank and begin dressing and grooming their fur like two small kittens. One stood up on its hind legs and appeared to sniff the air. Then both ambled slowly to the cattails and rushes at the water's edge and with their forepaws began to pull the plants toward them as they fed.

I could only guess that it might be these two venturesome young muskrats that would eventually wander away from the pond and become handsome brown-furred adults. All of the young that survive scatter in late summer to find new homes for themselves. Many dig burrows less than two hundred yards from the place where they were born. But four of the six in this litter in the dam would probably die, for only one-third of the young live into their first winter.

That summer I was able to trace with some definiteness the deaths of two of the young muskrats of the pond. One moonlit night in July I was sitting on the east bank listening to the booming calls of a pair of great horned owls on Laurel Hill. Their hunting territory included Muskrat Pond, and that night I had heard hungry young horned owls hissing from the edge of the woods. Then came the sounds of a struggle and sharp squeals. It was too far across the water for my light to reveal what was happening, but I heard a chattering scream of some animal as it was borne away through the air from the far edge of the pond. I had also heard that agonized cry from muskrats in marshes when I was a boy; it came when they had been mortally wounded by an otter or a mink. Once, in a pool by the side of a marsh I had seen a young muskrat seized by a snapping turtle and dragged soundlessly under. Death comes to many animals in silence, and one may learn of it only by inference from the slightest evidence. But to one who can read the calligraphy in the dust, a few tracks, scattered bits of fur, or even a trace of plucked feathers tell a vivid story.

◉ I had wondered for a long time about the homesite of the mink whose tracks I had seen along Muskrat Pond. I had suspected from its frequent trips there for frogs and crayfishes that it was a female with young, but though I had searched for her den I had not found it. One August night I moved silently along the road that leads to the pond. I love to walk in the darkness: it helps me approach night animals without frightening them and I have a feeling almost of weightlessness and of being suspended in this strange world so different from that of bright day. Odors and sounds are sharper at night, and after my eyes have become accustomed to the dark, I can see the pale, dusty road ahead well enough to walk soundlessly and without stumbling.

I switched on my light and shot the beam ahead. Two hundred feet away I saw a short-legged animal, lustrous black, crouching on the road. It was looking at me with blazing moon-green eyes out of a sharp little face. Its lithe body, about two feet long, almost touched the ground. Then it bounded off the road into a cornfield and disappeared.

The sweet odors of the corn and giant ragweed were all around me, but when I came to the place where the mink had been, I smelled its strange musky odor, stronger than that of a muskrat and almost like that of a skunk.

From glands in its groin, a muskrat drops a sweet scent that identifies its sex to others of its kind; a skunk discharges a fine spray in its own defense. I must have startled the mink, as it gives off its musk only when frightened or angry. There was a wildness in it, like that of some heavy Oriental perfume, and I found it a pleasing contrast to the sweet plant odors of the old field.

I had suspected that the mink lived along Morgan Creek; one September morning, at a time when the waters of the stream had died to a trickle and long stretches of muddy bars lay bare, I found the mink's trail. It led me for a quarter of a mile in and out of water and over low banks of cracked mud. At last it ended in an old muskrat burrow under the roots of an enormous sycamore by a shallow pool. The open mouth of the burrow was exposed above the water, and mink tracks led in and out of the hole, showing that it was much used. Again I smelled the musky mink odor. I leaned down and looked within. About a foot inside I saw a patch of gray fur and some bones recently cleaned of their flesh. They were all that remained of a young muskrat, and I knew then that the trail of at least one of the wandering young ones had ended there.

The June
Road

ℰ I have a naturalist's love for the road that winds from Muskrat Pond to the borders of Big Oak Woods. In June, the poet's month, I follow it for two miles southward, past fields of young green corn and rose hedges, past grassy ditches white with elderberry and Queen Anne's lace and trumpet creeper in scarlet flower. Cardinals and mockingbirds sing from the roadside thickets and bluebirds warble softly from the sky. In the early morning, when the dew sparkles on the grass, I hear the wild, sweet singing of the field sparrows and the first daylight calls of the quail.

In the heat of the ten o'clock forenoon, yellow-breasted chats *chuck,* whistle, and *churk* in the sunny hedges, and the small yellowthroats sing, *witch-a-wee! witch-a-wee! witch-a-wee!* from the fragrant fields of skullcap, daisies, and purple vetch. As I walk the warming road, I sometimes hear the slither of a harmless racer, or king, or garter, snake moving deeper into the grass, or the quick stir of a meadow mouse running from its nest.

But when I reach Big Oak Woods, I see and hear wild things that are not of the open fields. Ahead, the little ground lizards rustle the brown leaves as they scamper across the shaded road, and overhead, I see a flash of red, then hear the rich caroling of summer and scarlet tanagers. From deeper in the woods comes the loud drumming of a pileated wookpecker and its wild flickerlike call; the mellow trill of tree frogs; the scolding of a gray squirrel. High among the branches of the oaks, I see big yellow-and-black butterflies

drifting in the filtered sunlight and hear a murmuring of
bees from their hive in a hollow gum. . . .

It was there, along the west border of these woods
that I came to the end of a long, long trail—one that I had
begun as a young man almost a thousand miles to the north.
It had been a butterfly that had drawn me off the road into
Big Oak Woods: a rare black-and-white zebra swallowtail.
I had followed it only a little way when I saw a
birdlike nest in a bush. . . .

CHAPTER VII

Search for
the Golden
Mouse

૯ₐ At the edge of Big Oak Woods a sudden night breeze stirred the June thickets and swept through the forest of oaks and pines. With it I smelled the perfume of wild phlox, a fragrance that scented the Caroline woodland day and night. In the dusk I saw bats and moths emerge with the first darkness and flutter about soundlessly in the dying light. From nearby Willow Oak Swamp, I heard a barred owl call to the first stars. The night world of the old Mason Farm was beginning to awaken.

It was an hour before moonrise. Somewhere in the gloom of the thickets of Big Oak Woods, near the farm road where I stood, the elfin golden mice would soon creep from their nests to scamper about in the vines and shrubbery.

In my forty years as a naturalist, I had never seen a golden mouse. From all I had heard about it, it had seemed an elusive fairy of the Southern oak and pine forests, living from Virginia and Kentucky south to Florida and west to Texas, Arkansas, and Missouri. In a glistening coat of red-gold, and with white belly fur

and pink, handlike feet, this
one-ounce animal was said
to race about over the
twigs and branches of
its woodland home like
a miniature golden
tree squirrel. And it was
said to be the only wild
mouse in all of North
America that spends most
of its life in trees and shrubbery—
except for a red tree mouse of the Pacific coast.

In 1961, when I moved from New York State south to Chapel
Hill, North Carolina, I was for the first time living within the
realm of the golden mouse. During the next three years I spent
weeks crawling through thickets of greenbrier and honeysuckle in
search of its nests. Because it seldom descends to the ground, the
way to capture a golden mouse—I had been told—was to surprise
it in one of its homes that it builds in the forks of trees and shrubs.
Day after day I searched the woods and swamps around Chapel
Hill, poking gently into its snug retreats, then quickly encircling
the nests with my hands to prevent the escape of any occupants.
But not once did I find a golden mouse at home, although I
discovered more than sixty of its nests.

Now I stood at the edge of this North Carolina forest with a
new plan. There was another way that seemed to offer a remote
but hopeful chance of capturing a golden mouse. Perhaps it would
bring me my first sight of one.

In the darkness, under the woodland leaves by the side of the road, I had set my harmless traps. They were small corridors of aluminum in which I had scattered crumbled walnut kernels, mixed with peanut butter and oatmeal. If a golden mouse should descend from a shrub or tree to the ground and enter a trap in response to the odor of the bait, a small aluminum door would spring shut behind it.

Nothing is quite so exciting to a naturalist as the thought of capturing a live animal he has never seen. As I set the traps, my hands trembled in the glare of my flashlight.

I had come to the forest prepared to spend the night. I wanted to be a part of the golden mouse's world, if for only a few hours, and possibly to hear the snap of the metal door that would tell me one had entered one of my traps. I stretched out on an army cot under the sheltering canvas I pitched at the edge of the woods.

In the early dusk, the whippoorwills began to call, and soon the forest rang with their cries. Many were migrants, on their way north to New England and Canada. One alighted within ten feet of me and began its loud, rhythmic WHIP-*poor-will*, WHIP-*poor-will*, WHIP-*poor will* with the low *cluck* note before each phrase. The cry was so loud that, had a golden mouse entered one of my traps set only inches away, I could not have heard it. Presently the bird fell silent. Presumably it flew away, because I did not hear it again.

I first heard of the golden mouse in 1927. Naturalists knew very little about it at that time, although they had known of its existence for almost a century, ever since its discovery in Dismal

Swamp, Virginia. In 1831, Dr. Richard Harlan, a Philadelphia naturalist and physician, described in a technical journal the first golden mouse known to the scientific world. It was one of several sent to him by Thomas Nuttall, the eminent botanist of Harvard University. Nuttall had caught them in a nest under the bark of a tree in the swamp near Norfolk, Virginia. Following a common scientific practice of the times, of naming a newly discovered animal or plant for its collector, Dr. Harlan named the mouse in honor of Nuttall. In later years it was called the northern golden mouse, possibly because it had been discovered along the northern part of its range.

In 1927, the year I first heard of the golden mouse, Andrew L. Pickens, a naturalist who in future years was to become a friend of mine, discovered several near Troy, South Carolina, forty miles north of Augusta, Georgia. He caught a lone one in a birdlike nest it had built in a bush eight feet above the ground. Then he captured two more that were living together in a hollow tree nearby.

Pickens took the mice home to his room in a boarding house. They quickly became attached to Pickens and he to his immaculate pets. A young lady at the boarding house who ordinarily had a horror of mice was attracted to Pickens's small pets and even allowed them to crawl over her arms and hands. Apparently golden mice had the power not only to charm a naturalist but a woman who loathed mice. Who else had known and admired them?

Theodore Roosevelt, twenty-sixth President of the United

States, knew about them. In 1914, in a letter of reminiscences to his friend Henry Fairfield Osborn, he wrote:

As a boy I worked in the Museum [The American Museum of Natural History, New York City] and . . . remember skinning some rather reddish, white-footed mice I thought were golden mice and was disappointed to find they were not . . .

In December 1938, I began my search for the golden mouse when I made my first naturalist's trip to the South. On the way to Florida, I stopped at my father's old plantation home in South Carolina to take some photographs—and to search for golden mice. Although I hunted for days in the haunts of the pinewoods sparrow and wild turkey, looking in old birds' nests and in hollow trees, I found not one. Yet, not far from there, John James Audubon and his naturalist friend the Reverend John Bachman of Charleston had found them. During their field studies of wild mammals of the United States, they wrote that a South Carolina golden mouse had run about in an oak tree so swiftly that they had been forced to shoot it in order to capture it for their scientific collection. It was an animal new to them. In 1841, in their three-volume published work about the mammals of North America, they named and described it as the "orange-colored mouse," the beautiful creature which scientists now call the southern golden mouse.

A whisperlike stir in the leaves of the nearby woodland floor brought me quickly back from my thoughts about the early history of the golden mouse. I raised slightly from my cot to listen.

Perhaps I had heard a golden mouse, or possibly a shrew, but no snap of a trap door sounded in the night. I lay flat again, my face to the moonlit sky, listening sharply.

That morning, about fifteen feet from where I lay on my cot, I had found the nest of a golden mouse. That was why I had set my traps on the woodland floor closeby. Using plant stems, the small builders of the football-sized nest had lashed it to the fork of a sumac tree about eight feet above the ground. They had built the nest out of dry grasses that they must have gathered from on open field and the bark of wild-grape vines that hung like shaggy brown ropes from a giant tree at the edge of Big Oak Woods. In finishing it off, they had thatched the roof with the leaves of dogwood, oak, and wild cherry. These were woven so tightly that the roof would shed water and keep the mice inside warm and dry.

The nest had not been there the week before. I thought of how hard the mice must have worked, night after night, to build it and of the dangers they must have risked, running about in the field and in Big Oak Woods to gather their materials. They left a small round opening in each side of the nest. I learned that, upon the approach of anyone bent on finding them at home, they usually rush out of these openings, drop to the ground, and dash away. Perhaps that was why they had always eluded me. Hearing me approach through the dry leaves, they were gone before I ever could get close enough to see them.

In looking into many of their nests, I discovered that golden mice build two kinds. One is smaller than the other, a summer nest in which the female bears her two or three pink-skinned young; the pair of mice always build this nest in the thorniest, densest thickets of greenbrier, whose thorns tear one's flesh and clothing. They build a larger one in shrubs and even high in trees, up to fifty feet above the ground; in it the golden mice store their harvests of seeds. In these "dining room" nests, individual mice, pairs, or entire families from surrounding golden mouse territories gather to eat like tiny people at a church supper.

The nest in the sumac nearby was one of these miniature dining halls. In it I had found the shells of five thousand seeds of sumac, one of their favorites, the split shells of wild cherries, and the halved seeds of dogwood and of greenbrier. Most astonishing of all, I had found there the husks of the tiniest of all seeds in these North Carolina fields and woodlands—those of bedstraw and wild clovers. Some of them are no larger than the head of a pin. When I gathered the seed remains in my hands, I marveled at what must be the wonderful dexterity of the golden mouse's small forepaws. For it can manipulate these smallest of seeds as deftly as a gray squirrel can turn a hickory nut about in its forepaws. The halves of the shells showed that each seed must have been held, squirrel-like, in a golden mouse's forepaws before it had been opened. Then, with its teeth, the mouse had slit the seed down its sides to get at the sweet green food within.

Later I learned that the golden mouse, during its evolution, has evolved cheek pouches. Within these each mouse carries back to its nest a small load of seeds. The capacity of its cheek pockets saves it many trips to the ground or out on tree branches.

⁂ The early reddish moon had risen higher and had changed to a silver orb in the sky. From my cot in the shadowed woodland border, I looked down the grass-grown road of the abandoned farm to the weedy fields that lay like old silver under the moon. Within the woods, long shafts of white light fell on the forest floor. The chirps of a few early-season crickets broke the silence, but not sufficient to mask the whisper of tiny feet stirring the leaves. Possibly the golden mice were searching for seeds to carry back to their food storage nest. This was always dangerous: a pair of gray foxes that lived in Willow Oak Swamp often hunted along this woodland border and stalked the brown meadow mice of the open fields. And in the beam of my powerful light, I had seen raccoons and opossums traveling the roads and woodland trails at night in search of small animal life.

The whippoorwills had begun to call again in the distance. I fell asleep. Suddenly a tremendous guttural cry split the night. I awakened with a cold chill of fear and leaped from my cot. The cry came again: WHOO-WHOO-WHOO! WHO-COOKS-FOR-YOU-A-L-L! A barred owl had chosen the dead stub of a willow oak over my head from which to shatter the night with its booming cries. At my quick movement, it flapped silently out of the tree. I saw it briefly as it soared over the moonlit field, then it was gone.

Not a sound broke the silence now. The owl's cries had probably frightened every mouse, shrew, and other small creature into frozen quiet and had caused the golden mice to shiver close together in their nests. Owls are hereditary enemies of mice and catch enormous numbers of them in the night.

I looked at my watch. It was four o'clock in the morning, and I still had heard no sound of one of the doors of my traps snapping in the darkness. I did not dare move into the woodland to inspect the traps for fear of frightening away any golden mouse that might have been near. I went back to sleep.

Suddenly, from close by, I heard a sharp snap of metal. At the moment the sound pierced the air, I awakened. The moon had set, and beyond the woodland, the first faint light of day glowed in the east. I did not hesitate now. I had to know if I had caught a golden mouse. I picked up my spotlight, switched it on, and stepped cautiously into the woods. I swung the beam toward the leafy base of the sumac tree in which the golden mice had their nest. I could clearly see the place where I had covered my two small traps with brown leaves.

Carefully I uncovered the first one. The trap was unsprung. I moved to the next one and swept away the leaves. The trap door was shut. My heart pounded as I picked up the trap. Something alive inside was making quick movements.

I had brought with me a large cardboard carton. I held the trap over the carton and opened the trap door. Nothing came out, but when I shook it a small animal dropped out and alighted on all fours in the bottom of the carton. In the beam of my light I looked down on the daintiest, most fairylike creature I had ever seen. It looked up into the light out of large, dark, shining eyes, its long whiskers quivering on each side of a delicate pink nose. It was sitting up with its forefeet held in front of its snow-white breast, like a tiny squirrel. The fur on its back was red-gold. I was looking at my first golden mouse!

For one hundred and ten days the golden mouse shared my cottage in Chapel Hill. I kept him in a large cage in which I had put small branches of shrubs. They provided him with a miniature forest such as he had known in the wild. In a corner I placed a snug golden mouse nest that I had found in a greenbrier thicket at the edge of a swamp. A pair of golden mice had built it of grasses and had lined it with milkweed down that they gleaned from seed pods high on the plant stalks. For additional softness, into the downy lining they had woven the molted feathers of cardinals and catbirds that share the golden mouse's leafy summer thickets.

Within twenty-four hours my golden mouse was racing over the branches of his new home as though he had known the place all his life. Traveling swiftly, he ran over the tiny tree trails like a diminutive squirrel. Sometimes he would stop on a branch no thicker than a lead pencil and stand up on it as he steadied himself by holding to the branch with his long tail.

The golden mouse slept in his nest most of the day. At night he stole out and came to the little glass food dish in which I had scattered wild millet and sunflower seeds with bits of cheese crackers and slices of apple that he had always eaten by morning.

During the night, his cracking of seeds often awakened me. I would get up and switch on the light to talk with him while he sat in a corner listening and watching me with an expression of inscrutable, ageless wisdom in his dark eyes.

Sometimes, when he tired of my talk, he darted to the tube of the glass water vial I had hung in his cage and drank with rapid lapping motions of his small pink tongue. One time when I drove to New York City he traveled with me and lived for a while in a Manhattan apartment.

At first he allowed me to handle him and would crawl curiously over my hands and arms. But gradually, day by day, instead of becoming tamer, he grew wilder until I knew at last I must return him to his home forest.

It was near sunset of a hazy day in October when I drove my car over the old farm road to the place where the golden mouse nest still hung in the fork of the sumac. The yellow leaves of the willow oaks cast a canopy of light along the edge of the woods, and the sweet smell of the last wild asters filled the air. At the base of the tree, I opened the cage. The golden mouse did not hesitate. In a flash he darted under the carpet of brown leaves. There was a faint rustle, then silence. He was gone.

*The Travelway
from the Swamp*

It is one thousand of my booted strides from the place where I released the golden mouse at the edge of Big Oak Woods east to Morgan Creek and Willow Oak Swamp. Within my memory, the swamp had always been a refuge for raccoons, and its long, long history, written in the sizes and ages of its trees, told me that it had been so for at least two centuries, possibly before Mark Morgan came to this land. But it was the Creek—Morgan's Creek—which feeds the swamp and belongs to the vast geological past, that I followed in most of my studies of the raccoons.

From the sky, looking down on gray winter, a passing hawk might see Morgan Creek as a silver ribbon flowing eastward across the land. At the northeast corner of the Mason Farm it turns south, and after a twisting mile through open fields it glides into Willow Oak Swamp. There its shining face is a shattered mirror, splintered by the limbs and crowns of naked trees. Some of these swamp giants, wind-torn from a thousand violent storms, have hollows in their trunks in which generations of raccoons have made their homes.

Through the years, while the aging swamp became their refuge and a fortress against winter cold, the hungry raccoons hunted the creek for the bounty of its waters. Leaving their dens after dark, they foraged in a stream that for centuries had been their travelway through the creek flatlands and past the open fields to the west. Sometimes, depending on the ripeness or availability of the foods of the season, the raccoons left the creek.

In the dark, they shuffled along the farm roads, the wet ditches, and the woodland trails, smelling and feeling of anything that might be food. Their forefeet, exquisitely sensitive to touch, grasped with lightning speed the startled mouse, the frog, crayfish, grasshopper, or beetle before it could escape the small black paws. And what their sensitive *feet* did not find, the raccoons discovered with their *noses.*

Lifting their faces into the night, they sifted the currents of air for the sweet-smelling wild plums and purple grapes in the woodland thickets or the tender green corn in the fields of summer. But it was along Morgan Creek that I was always sure of finding their trails, especially in the season of low water. Then, in July and in August, I easily followed the marks of their paws on the exposed muddy banks. Like the human imprints of babies' hands and feet, their tracks crisscrossed the water's edge and wound through the sands of the last shallow pools.

CHAPTER VIII

The Raccoons of Morgan Creek

&ᴆ Each spring I watched green leaf-fire spread over the wooded banks of Morgan Creek. It began on the ground, in the beds of violets and chickweed, then leaped to the thickets of honeysuckle and elderberry, and on upward into the trees that towered above. There it opened a green umbrella in the crowns of the elms and ashes and tall, white-barked sycamores and shaggy river birches. By summer the green archway had closed. Not until gray November, when the winds had stripped away its last golden leaves, would the creek be open to the skies again.

Beneath the jade roof of April, the stream dimpled and flowed through sunshine and shadow. Stealing through the streamside thickets, I saw wood ducks swimming on its surface and painted turtles crawl from the green waters to sun themselves on the trunks of trees that had fallen into the creek. Lying on a grassy bank, I watched the red sunfishes build their gravel nests on the yellow stream bottom and the little water striders skating over the surface.

One April day, while I walked under the trees on the high stream bank, I surprised a gray fox that had not heard my coming because of the roaring wind. It turned its sharp face toward me briefly as its sunlit body and bushy tail disappeared into the shadows of a honeysuckle thicket. The fox was there to hunt, possibly for the brown muskrats whose tracks and burrows I had seen along the stream banks. But it was the tracks of the raccoons that I followed most, because it was their earth trails that told me much about their adventures. In time, however, I learned far more by watching the raccoons themselves at night.

When the last golden light fades in the fields and deep dusk rises out of Willow Oak Swamp, they begin to stir in their dens. Barred owls are beginning to call as the raccoons first look out of their tree hollows at oncoming night. Their rounded furry ears point forward then back, catching every sound—the snap of a twig under a deer's hoof, the far baying of a distant hound, the lightest tread of a passing fox, the faintest squeak of a shrew or a mouse. As they peer dark-eyed from their black-masked faces, they lift their slender muzzles to sniff the night. They have nothing to fear from the barred owls that nest in the broken tops of the old oaks, but their nightly exodus is not without stealth and caution. The Edwards Mountain bobcat, capable of killing raccoons, hunts there, and men with their guns and dogs come into the swamp from the forest that extends for miles to the south. Only in spring and in summer are they safe from the hunters. Then they are protected by law.

By dark many of the raccoons have left their dens and have started down the rough-barked trees. Gripping the trunks with their five-clawed front and hind feet, some descend headfirst like squirrels. Others back down slowly, clutching the trees and looking below like cautious children. When they touch the swamp floor, their night-roving has begun.

᪇ My tracking of raccoons traveling overland out of Willow Oak Swamp was always fragmentary, except when snow lay on the ground. For seven years, from spring until fall, and through much of the Southern winters, I followed the trails of hundreds of raccoons over the Mason Farm: from the small young, moving about with their nine- to twelve-pound mothers, to the largest roving males that must have weighed fifteen or twenty pounds. After the raccoons moved out of deep dust or mud, I soon lost their trails in the leafy woods or on hard ground where their feet made no impression. But there was one raccoon whose tracks I followed one winter day for half a mile to its den at the edge of Willow Oak Swamp that left one of the most exciting trails I had ever seen.

The usual size of a raccoon's front feet, from its heels to the ends of its toes, is two to three inches; the hind feet, about four. The tracks left by the front feet of this one were three and one half inches long; the hind feet, six inches! He was the largest raccoon I had ever followed and, eventually, when I saw him, I estimated his weight at thirty pounds. I saw his tracks all during my first year on the Mason Farm, and from his distinctive trail I got to know him well.

Ordinarily I have no names for my small animal friends living wild and free. But this raccoon I called The Big One, and he would always be that to me—to the end of his trail and surely to the end of mine. Along Morgan Creek, I often saw his tracks, intermingled with those of other raccoons. Many of them gave way before him as I discovered by watching them at night—all, that is, except one female with three cubs which I correctly guessed was his mate. His tracks dwarfed those of his family and pressed far deeper in the mud, testifying to his unusual weight.

I have known many raccoons in the wild that have shown me they were smart and capable of shrewd animal reasoning. These were animals trailed by dogs—with which I joined when the prize for the hunter was simply in the chase and the reward for the raccoon, its freedom. A wise old raccoon is as clever as a fox in breaking its trail against following hounds.

One autumn night in Pennsylvania, with several companions and four dogs, I followed a raccoon that climbed a stone wall and ran along it for a considerable distance before it descended to the ground. In Maryland, another broke its trail and left our hounds puzzled when it climbed a rail fence and walked along the top until it came to a stream. There it descended to the ground and waded in water until it had left the dogs far behind. Some raccoons will climb a tree to break their fresh scent on the ground, and before the dogs have arrived will leap to another and, flattened on a limb high in the treetop, hide from the hunters. Others will climb a tree near a stream or pond, then drop to the water—which leaves no raccoon odor for the pursuing hounds.

Harmless as these chases were, I long ago gave them up, for they must have brought discomfort and fear to the pursued animals. And if the dogs caught up with a raccoon on the ground, they would attack it and try to kill it.

One night, near Chapel Hill, North Carolina, hunters with their hounds trailed a raccoon that ran only a short distance before it climbed a tree. When one of the men in the party ascended the big oak to get a close look at the quarry, he was astonished to find not an adult but four baby raccoons sitting in the outer branches. When he flashed his light on them, they stared back curiously and without fear. Two of them were close together on the same branch. While the light was on them, one of the young raccoons turned to the other and began to lap at its ears. Both acted as though they were alone, with no threat of danger near. They were too young to understand that men and dogs could be their deadly enemies.

The mother raccoon had disappeared. Apparently, after leading her young ones to the tree, she had leaped to the ground and had run ahead to leave a trail that would entice the dogs away. The men called off their dogs and left the young raccoons in the tree, sure in their knowledge that the mother's devotion to her family would bring her back to lead them safely to the home den.

Ingenious as the wild ones are, it requires pet raccoons to show the full capabilities of their kind. Put to tests that never face a wild raccoon, they learn to open screen and refrigerator doors; to retrieve food put in almost inaccessible places by their owners to test raccoon intelligence; to remove jar caps; pull corks from bottles; unfasten the latches of cages; and turn doorknobs. All of this they do with their handlike forepaws if the lure that drives them to problem solving is something they like to eat.

A raccoon's intelligence is greater than a cat's and is second to that of a monkey. Raccoons are immensely curious and agile; they also have large appetites and seem always hungry. Perhaps they use their wits best in food getting and in escaping their enemies, which accounts for their success as a species and high rate of survival. Yet, they also show understanding in situations in which food has no part. I was to learn this from The Big One, the oversize raccoon of Morgan Creek. He seemed to have all the brain power common to his kind, but in one incident along his trail, he had apparently used judgment that must have come from long experience.

One October morning, during the first year that I knew him, I came upon The Big One's tracks in the dust of a road that paralleled the creek. He had been traveling westward in the night, and I had followed his trail for only a few hundred yards when I saw that he must have paused in his shuffling gait. His tracks showed that he had brought all four feet together as he halted. Ahead I saw the S-shaped trail of a heavy-bodied snake that had rested on the road, then crossed it in the night. The thickness of its body markings in the dust, abruptly tapering to the outline of a short, thin tail, told me that the trail had been made by a copperhead, the only kind of poisonous snake on the Mason Farm. The coolness of the October nights must have stimulated it to move from the lowlands of Morgan Creek toward its hibernating place among the rocks of a nearby ridge.

The confrontation between the raccoon and the copperhead appeared to have been sudden, as their trails seemed to have converged at the same time. Then I saw from The Big One's tracks that he had turned away and had gone around the snake before resuming his course westward on the dusty road.

Raccoons often eat snakes that are not poisonous. Had The Big One some way of knowing that this was a deadly one? Or was he simply not hungry enough to attack the snake? I had only the trails in the dust to tell me what must have been only a part of the story.

The heat of the oncoming August night hung suffocatingly over Morgan Creek. From my place in an old chair bottom that I had nailed in the crotch of a sycamore that slants over the stream, I could hear the whisper of the barely moving waters below. The creek was at its lowest of the year, with only a trickle running over the low dam that bridges it. It was dusk, the awakening time of the raccoons, but they would not be moving along the stream to hunt for at least half an hour.

Those that had denned in Big Oak Woods or on Laurel Hill might arrive first because they had not as far to travel as those in

Willow Oak Swamp. Others might come from even closer, for a raccoon—except when it is in its winter den—may use a different bed every day. Wherever it ends its hunting, and whether at midnight or at four in the morning, it will find a sleeping place nearby. Those that do not find a hollow tree may crawl into a hollow log, a fox's ground burrow, or even make a bed in the cattails of an open marsh. Many rotate their hunting areas and sleeping places from night to night, or from day to day, and eventually return to the same dens at a later time.

Tonight many of the raccoons would again be attracted to Morgan Creek. Six weeks of drought had parched the land and had shrunken the wide stream in places to a brook's width. I had chosen my perch on the sycamore from a dozen other giants because a large limb of the tree extended over a pool. And that pool in spring was the deepest of any along Morgan Creek. But now it was so shallow that raccoons could wade in it and hunt for the crayfishes that in high waters were inaccessible to them. I had seen crayfishes by the hundreds on the pool bottom, and the trails of raccoons were all along the muddy banks, showing that it was a favorite raccoon feeding place.

From the southwest I heard a faint rumble of thunder and saw a flare of lightning in the sky. The rain, if it should come, was still far away and the raccoons would be out before it arrived. And if the rain came, it would bring greenness back to the brown fields and a rush of cool waters to the streams and to the parched floor of Willow Oak Swamp.

I shifted about until I had settled myself comfortably in the tree, then flashed the beam of my miner's headlight downstream. It was eight o'clock and almost dark. In the white light I saw hundreds of small moths fluttering about. A large imperial moth rose out of the darkness into the light, its eyes glowing ruby-red. It disappeared in the night.

I snapped off the light. A whippoorwill began its loud calling from nearby, and I heard the hum of the mosquitoes that hung like a cloud around my head. I had come prepared and had sprayed my arms and clothing with a mosquito repellent which kept them away. I sat motionless, listening sharply for the sound I wanted to hear. It came, a light splash from upstream, followed by a low purring note.

I waited for a few moments, then flashed my headlight up the creek. At first I saw only the muddy bank and a sand bar, but on turning my head slightly, the beam lighted the edge of the shallow pool not more than one hundred feet away. I saw an adult raccoon wading in the water with his back slightly arched and his tail raised. He was moving ahead and reaching under the water with his forefeet. So vigorously did he manipulate his sensitive paws and fingers that I saw his furry shoulders rolling with the motion. When the beam of my light first played over him, he turned quickly toward me. I saw a red glow from each eye, a reflection kindled by my powerful light. The flash came from the layer of refractive cells behind his eye retinas. Then I saw a flash of green as the raccoon shifted his eyes away and my light struck them at a different angle. He had turned his back on me to resume his fishing.

ಆ In flashing my light on and off raccoons at night, I discovered that the light did not disturb them if I remained silent. But at my slightest sound—the snap of a twig or even my lightest footfall—they ran off into the darkness. That is why I had chosen to watch them from a tree. There I could sit in silence and also be high enough above the stream that they might not catch my scent readily and possibly be frightened away.

ಆ The raccoon, which appeared by its large size to be a male, brought up a crayfish in one paw, gave it a quick bite to disable it, then began to eat it, tail first. I could hear the cracking of his teeth on the shell of the crayfish and saw their flashing whiteness as he fed with his lips drawn back to the gums. Raccoons have forty teeth, and they seem to use them all as they chew their food thoroughly, not gulping it as a dog or a fox will.

The raccoon had been feeding for about ten minutes, during which he caught three or four crayfishes, all of which he ate in the water. Then he brought up a large one and climbed out of the pool to the top of a low rock at the water's edge. He sat up to eat his catch.

Suddenly he stopped feeding and turned his face toward my

light. His eyes were glowing and his ears were pointed toward me. I had not made a sound, but now I heard something moving in the water below me. I turned the light downward. My heart leaped at what I saw. It was the largest raccoon I had ever seen, and I knew that it must be The Big One.

He stopped and turned to look up into my light. Again I saw the glitter of reflected eye red, then of green as he turned away. He shuffled up the stream with a rolling motion, his head lifted and his ears pointed sharply forward. I knew by his actions that he had seen or heard the other raccoon feeding on the rock. As he drew near it, I heard both animals growl deeply. The raccoon on the low rock had dropped his crayfish and stood with his back slightly arched. He bared his teeth, which gleamed whitely in the light.

The Big One had slowed his pace and was snarling menacingly. When he drew near the rock, he, too, arched his back and stretched upward until he appeared taller than his rival. Both faced each other not four feet apart. Their ears were laid back and they were growling ferociously.

The raccoon on the rock was the first to move off, but he did not back away from The Big One. He stepped down into the water without any sign of fear. Then he turned downstream with slow dignity to continue his night hunt. The Big One watched him go but did not follow.

I saw now that there would be no clash between them. Each had asserted himself without fighting. In their night-hunting, I had seen this intolerance between raccoons before. It keeps them spread out and allows them to make efficient use of their food supply. In a way, the bluff of each had been as effective as fighting; neither animal risked death or disablement from the other.

Then I saw a mother raccoon with three half-grown young ones come out of the darkness. They were on the bank opposite the place where The Big One was slowly moving about in the water. She was purring loudly—a throaty note that seemed to reassure her young and to keep them close to her.

She came to the edge of the pool, waded in, and the young raccoons followed. Reaching forward with her paws under the water, she searched for a crayfish, caught one, and held it to her mouth. The three young raccoons were also groping under the shallow water with their forepaws, imitating exactly the actions of their mother. But I noticed that they did not wade deeply. They hunched their small backs as though afraid of getting their bodies wet and raised their black-ringed tails well above the water. Occasionally they stopped and revolved their shoulders as they slithered their paws about on the bottom of the pool. Two of them caught crayfishes, but the mother had eaten several before her young ones had seized their first.

I was so fascinated by the behavior of the young raccoons that I had forgotten about The Big One. Now I heard him utter a low, snoring sound. I turned my light to the north edge of the pool at the place where I had seen him last. He had climbed the low rock and was squatting there on his haunches like a small bear. His front feet dangled limply in front of him over the edge of the rock, the long, slender fingers clearly discernible in the beam of my light. He was intently watching the female and her young.

Was his snoring note a warning to the female and her family to leave the pool? At the time, I knew little about the social behavior of raccoons or I would have known better. As I was to find out, all adult raccoons give way before mothers with their young at feeding places. But what was the meaning of the snoring sound?

The Big One had dropped into the water. The female moved slowly across the pool toward him. He met her part way out in the water, still uttering his low note. Now I knew they were mates. His semigrowl was an assurance to the female of his sociability, not a threat to her as I had supposed.

The male reached down and mouthed her shoulders. Then he turned away and yawned. The female started downstream followed by her young. The Big One turned and moved along with them, but he remained on the opposite side of the pool. Within a few minutes all of the raccoons had vanished in the darkness beyond reach of my light.

I had learned something about raccoon family relationships. But I think I had also learned why The Big One had been so aggressive toward the lone male that occupied the pool just before he arrived. The big fellow had not been establishing feeding rights to the pool, but had been asserting his protection over his female. Male raccoons are promiscuous in their breeding, but the females, once they have chosen a mate for the season, usually will not accept another.

I looked at the illuminated dial of my watch. It was nine o'clock, and my legs had stiffened from my sitting for an hour, motionless in the tree chair. The storm had arrived and sharp flashes of lightning played overhead. As I descended the few feet from the tree crotch to the ground, I heard the patter of first rain in the leafy crowns of the trees. By the time I had walked the quarter mile to the concrete dam that bridges the stream, I felt pelting drops on my face and smelled the sweet freshness of the storm. The wind was rising, and as I got into my car parked on the road near the creek, I heard it roaring through the trees. Then came the downpour.

෨ I was deeply intrigued by what I had learned of the social habits of some of the raccoons of Morgan Creek. All that summer and into early autumn I watched them at night, as often as I could. I learned that more raccoons were out on dark nights; fewer on bright moonlit nights. And I discovered that the attraction between the male raccoon and his mate seems to be mutual, but that she is less demonstrative than he. She will accept his leadership while hunting, but at times she maintains an aloofness or dissociation from him. This suggested that she was less dependent on him for companionship than he was upon her. I also learned that all raccoons, except family groups, travel singly—usually *downstream*—and upon meeting are irritable and intolerant of each other. However, there is a strong attraction between mated pairs. They usually stay within fifty feet of each other while fishing and I never saw them quarrel.

I heard raccoons utter many sounds in the night: the low growl-purr of a mother to her young; the throaty, somewhat muffled snore or growl of recognition between pairs; the fierce hiss and snort that is a bluffing challenge to each other to fight; the bedlam of fierce explosive snarls and growls of two unsociable raccoons upon meeting.

The meaning of another call I heard from raccoons I have never been able to explain, unless it might be a croon of contentment. It is a rising and falling cry that resembles the soft, quavering whistle of a screech owl. Once, during the day, I heard a raccoon scream loudly in Big Oak Woods, perhaps in rage upon meeting another of its kind. It kept squalling for some time, then I heard low growls followed by silence.

I had seen and studied the behavior of single raccoons and of family groups. But what of their behavior when many of them are drawn together? How would an assemblage of raccoons act, especially when gathered at a single feeding place? I had always kept a winter feeding station for birds in my back yard. Why not a feeding station for raccoons somewhere in Willow Oak Swamp?

An old, one-room shack stands within two hundred feet of the north edge of the swamp. It had once housed a recluse—a man who had hunted the land long before I came to Chapel Hill. I had passed it many times in my travels along Morgan Creek, but had never thought that I might have a use for it someday. After my first brief inspection, I had never gone inside it again. In winter, the wind sometimes whistled the loneliness of the place as I passed.

The roof of the shack had partly fallen in, but the walls inside were patched and covered with tattered tar paper that had once assured some shelter from cold for the man who had lived there. Young sweet gums, arrow-straight, had grown out from the edge of the swamp and up to the door, which sagged on one hinge. The lone window facing the swamp had only a single pane of cracked glass, but with new panes and repairs to the inside walls, the shack would do. It would serve as a hiding place from which I could watch the raccoons.

An old table stood inside near the window. Beyond it, against the back wall, an old, battered, stuffed chair would offer a place to sit. I repaired the window glass and put a new hinge on the door so that I could close it against the cold. Then I put the chair close to the window. I could sit there in comfort with a good view outside the building.

I bought a portable oil stove and put it near the chair. I was now ready to spend my first nights in the hideaway. But before starting my nightly watch, I had to be sure that the raccoons could be attracted to the place.

I decided to bait an area in the front yard that had once been a garden plot. It was only about thirty feet from the window, close enough to the shack for me to see it clearly and in detail. I bought some shelled corn and in the November dusk spread it over the bare ground. Then I scratched the earth deeply all around the twenty-foot-square feeding place. The roughened ground would be my guest book. It would record for me the trail of any visiting animal and I could read its name by the signature of its tracks.

The next morning I returned to the feeding area. Not one raccoon track could I find, but the crows had been there early in the morning and the opossums during the night. I raked the earth again until I had smoothed away the tracks, then I replenished the feeding place with corn. Although I went back the next morning, and the next, I found not a trace of a raccoon. I was disappointed, but I did not give up hope that they would come; I was sure that the raccoons simply had not found the place, and were not avoiding it. They had probably been attracted to a supply of food elsewhere.

On the fourth day, at dusk, I spread an additional layer of shelled corn on the ground to replace that eaten by the crows, the opossums, and a lone gray fox whose tracks I had seen there. The November day had been mild; the temperature, 65°. By late afternoon it had dropped to 36°. There was no wind. The night promised to be one of still, sharp cold, but one that would not keep the raccoons in their dens. The next morning I found their trails all over the feeding area. Most of the corn was gone. The raccoons had been there, and now I was ready to watch.

That night, just before dark, I entered the old shack. I lighted the oil stove. Then I sat down in the chair by the window. I wore my miner's headlight over a woolen cap and had wrapped myself in two blankets against the bite of the cold. I had brought sandwiches and had just finished my cold supper in the darkness when I heard a slight sound beyond the window.

I switched on my head lamp. In the beam of light I saw a small, pale-gray opossum. It was darting nervously about at the edge of the feeding area, and its swift movements were nothing like those of the slow-moving, sluggish opossums I had seen by day. It stopped and turned. In the light its dark eyes were glittering and the hair was raised high from its head and back. Then it ran away into the swamp and disappeared.

Now came a gathering of raccoons such as I had ever seen before. For two hours—from seven to nine o'clock—I saw twenty-four. The first to arrive at the feeding area were young raccoons about a year old. They had long ago been weaned, were on their own and hungry as young bears. And into the circle of yearlings came family groups. Each mother led her cubs of the year, which followed closely at her sides. During the first six months of their lives the cubs are dominated completely by the parent.

At one time I counted four mothers: one with one cub, two with three cubs each, and one with four. The mothers with young fed amiably as a group over a six-foot circle in the middle of the feeding place. And I noticed that the mothers tolerated the yearlings as did other adult raccoons when they joined the group later in the night. They all kept their noses to the ground, eating hungrily and with great concentration.

By ten o'clock most of the mothers with their cubs had arrived, and some had departed by then, presumably to return to the home den. Now the large adult raccoons—without young—began to appear. Most of them came, not singly, but in pairs or groups of three to five. I was soon to discover the reason for it.

I noticed from the beginning that adult raccoons that came alone were threatened by the feeding group and soon driven away. But two or more adults arriving together could shuffle into the circle of feeding animals with confidence. It was their united front that forced their acceptance by the others; however, it was only one animal of the entering group that acted aggressively, as though *it* were the spokesman for its companions. Snarling, with ears laid back and shoulder fur bristling, it made gestures just short of fighting that caused those in the feeding group to turn away and allow the new group's entry into the circle. I saw, however, that once inside the larger group, each group remained together as it fed, as though it needed to do so to maintain its security.

While feeding and moving about, both adult and yearling raccoons gave way before a mother with her young. She dominated them all except the other family groups with which she appeared to be equal in her social standing.

Most of the families left the feeding area by midnight, and only rarely did I see one arrive after one o'clock in the morning. Late-feeding raccoons came from 1:30 a.m. to about 3:30 a.m., then their visits dropped off sharply. I saw no raccoons at the feeding place after 5:30 in the morning.

All through the winter, for three days each week, I continued to change my habits: I slept by day and watched the raccoons of Willow Oak Swamp by night. Gradually, I began to see a pattern in their behavior that was tied closely to the weather.

Raccoons were active during the winter nights if the temperature remained in the 30's or was higher. But with below-freezing cold, when it dropped into the 20's or lower, no raccoons came to the feeding area. Apparently they remained comfortably in their dens.

Snow had the same effect on them; they were far more likely to go into their winter sleep if cold weather was accompanied by a storm. One January night I saw a few raccoons at the feeding place when snow began to fall at midnight. Most of the raccoons had disappeared by that time, but some of them continued to feed until their backs were white with the drifting flakes. Then they, too, turned and like small, furry ghosts, slipped away into the still whiteness of the night.

In late January and early February I began to see a change in the temperaments of the raccoons. In the feeding circle, they showed increasing irritability at being close together. They snarled, squealed, and growled ferociously, and fights broke out. Their behavior was strikingly unlike the relative amiability they had shown in autumn and early winter. At that time, mere threats were sufficient to make one group acceptable to another. Now even the raccoons in small social groups were beginning to quarrel violently among themselves. They were so strife-ridden that I was not surprised when, by mid-February, the raccoons no longer came to the feeding area. There had been so much fighting that they seemed unable to settle down to eat. Besides, other natural foods were becoming available. Frogs and turtles had come out of hibernation in ponds and streams, and in the warming fields, crickets and grasshoppers were stirring and mice easier for the raccoons to catch with the snow gone and the ground thawing. But even with available natural food, the irritation of the raccoons upon meeting continued to rise. The breeding season had come and males were increasingly intolerant of each other as they traveled long distances in the night, going in and out of dens in their search of receptive females.

Strangely, that winter I had not seen The Big One at the feeding place. I had looked for him, straining my eyes at the sight of every large raccoon, but in all the nights that I watched, not one was the towering animal I had seen that summer night along Morgan Creek.

On January 19, I awakened to a storm that had begun early that morning. Because bad weather had been predicted, I had not gone to the shack by Willow Oak Swamp, but slept in my cottage at Chapel Hill.

Outside I heard a rushing sound. When I opened my door, sleet hissed and crackled as ice particles struck the leafless trees and bounced off the hard ground. Within an hour this had changed to snow, which fell all day. By nightfall it was bitterly cold. No raccoons would be active until the storm was over and the temperature rising again.

By January 21 the sun shone warmly. At the Mason Farm the snow on the wide fields was melting as I trudged toward the shack by Morgan Creek. I found no raccoon tracks there nor did I expect to, but the trails of cottontail rabbits crisscrossed the snow in all directions. I went on into Willow Oak Swamp, following the creek and walking soundlessly through the white-blanketed woods. A Carolina wren suddenly burst into wild melody from a nearby thicket. In the trees ahead, a tufted titmouse whistled over and over its mellow double note, and in the distance I heard the long, rolling tattoo of a woodpecker drumming on dead wood. Two chickadees fluttered low over my head, uttering scolding notes.

I had traveled a mile into the heart of the swamp before I saw a break in the surface of the snow. It was the trail of some animal, and when I drew nearer, my heart leaped with the excitement of that January day a year before. The marks were the tracks of a raccoon, and looking down on them, they appeared even larger in the wet snow than they had in the mud of Morgan Creek. I was sure that this was the trail of The Big One. He had crossed the creek over a fallen tree, then had turned southward toward an enormous oak that towered ahead in the swamp.

I followed the trail, walking slowly and looking sharply at the big tree ahead. Then, on one of the uppermost branches that slanted outward toward the blue January sky, I saw the large raccoon. He was sprawled flat, his front and hind feet dangling

over the sides
of the branch. His
eyes were closed and his chin
was resting on the bark. And in that
moment I saw two smaller raccoons lower in the
giant tree. Each was in a separate crotch; each was
coiled with its face buried between its forepaws. All three
were asleep in the warm sunshine, oblivious to their world.

A warmth swept over me at the innocence of these sleeping animals; then dread, at their vulnerability. I might have been their enemy instead of being their friend. Completely disarmed, they were risking their lives for this moment of ease. Yet they were wild and free, and this must be freedom's way for them—taking the small comfort between terror and pain before the last sweet darkness and silence without end.

Insect Summer

و Summer belongs to the insects, and in the drowsy heat of July and August, when I walk southward over the brown road from Morgan Creek to Lone Field, I am never out of hearing of the buzzing of meadow grasshoppers, the whirring of Carolina locusts in flight, the rattling of the wings of wasps, the droning of bees at the old field flowers. Birds sing early. The awakening whistle of quail comes at dawn from the hedges, and in the cool, green woods, the redstarts, summer tanagers, and red-eyed vireos sing long before the heat waves shimmer over the road and the sun has burned away the morning mists. But it is the insects that proclaim high summer, and at noon of days when the temperature rises to more than 100° they are fiercely active.

In July, in the searing heat, the scissors-grinder cicadas sound their *ziz-z-zape! ziz-z-zape! ziz-z-zape!* and under the dazzling sun, the black solitary wasps, with their rapier stings, climb like graceful d'Artagnans over the roadside flowers of mountain mint. Golden-footed wasps also come to the pale flowers for nectar; others come like pirates to snatch away the white crab spiders that lie hidden, waiting to seize the delicate butterflies that visit the grape-scented, gray-white blooms. And so the drama of insect against spider and spider against insect is played out in the hearts of the summer flowers.

By mid-August the most terrible heat of the year lies over the Mason land. As I walked southward again, toward Lone Field, I can reach out and touch the ranks of first-flowering goldenrod by the roadside: the tall, elegant *altissima.* Beyond it, I see the rough, giant ragweed and the standing green corn—twelve feet tall—and the Johnson grass in purple flower. I feel smothered, walled in by the height and lushness of the plants. The air, sweet with their heavy fragrance, comes hot from the fields like a blast furnace, fierce and choking, yet healing to my lungs and perspiring flesh.

A sudden shower comes from a lone black cloud that has moved directly overhead. I lift my face to the silver rain and feel its cool sweetness, and hear the drops, like a million fingers, drumming the cornfield's leaves. As the cloud moves on, the patter of rain runs with it, across the field and away until it ceases. Then a fresh breeze stirs the tops of the corn, and the long leaves whisper as they touch, and the breeze dies, and they grow silent. The heat is here again, the sunlight blazing, the air silent and moist, the plants sparkling with fallen rain.

At a patch of swamp milkweed, I stop to watch a group of butterflies dancing over the lavender flowers—a great spangled fritillary; some yellow-and-black tiger swallowtails; and a pipe-vine swallowtail, exquisite in the metallic blue of its wings, with a circular scattering of white, like stars on a blue field.

Then I see them, at the milkweed, and can scarcely believe what I see there—four dainty hummingbird moths rising and falling in the warm air, their swift-beating wings like shadows at their sides, their long wirelike tongues dipping again and again into nectaries of the lavender flowers. They are smaller than the tiniest hummingbird and have greenish backs—like soft plush—with ruby-red bodies and black tail-parts. This is the day-flying moth *thysbe,* named for the Thisbe of Pyramus, covered with lovers' blood.

The moths hover at the flowers, delicate as fairies, and silver-spotted skipper butterflies come there and join them, with syrphus flies and bumblebees, all feeding in turn, in polite peace. Then I hear an angry buzz and see a robber fly, with its stiletto beak, alight on a milkweed stalk below the flowers. It perches there, head pointed upward, like a waiting hawk. But it makes no darting move at the soft-bodied moths, and soon speeds away.

When I move out of the sunlight and follow the brown road through the shaded woods, I leave the flower insects behind and see the dust baths of the quail, dug like small pockets in the old road. These are signs of the rust-colored birds I had come to see, in Lone Field ahead, and I think of the beginning of their story and of the time that I first got to know them, here at the edge of Laurel Hill Woods.

CHAPTER IX

The Lone Field Covey

හ The June sunshine lay warm on Lone Field and its curving rows of young corn. In the southwest corner of the Mason Farm and open to the sky, this is a silent place, high above the wide fields and woods far below. Its five acres, almost surrounded by forest, might have been cut from the pines and oaks by Mark Morgan himself—the pioneer who, with his wife, settled this part of the land two centuries ago.

Along the field's south border, the fragrant needles of pines glisten in the morning sunlight, and along the field's western edge, the gray-green woods of Laurel Hill rise to meet the horizon of blue sky. Leading north from Lone Field, through a dense oak woods, a narrow road, like a thin brown line, connects it with the rest of the farm.

At the field's north border, a pile of large stones lies scattered in a grassy clearing under two giant oaks. It marks the place where an old house stood that long ago moldered away. At the north edge of the clearing, thickets of young cedars and pines advance a little farther into the grass each year—the first line of the encroaching woods.

But the borders of Lone Field are still open, with the young trees beaten back at the ends of the rows by the plow and the harrow of the farmer who annually sows his crop of corn there. These edges are thick with tall weeds and grasses and patches of wild blackberry and dewberry, still unconquered by the forest. It is a place of loneliness, and of wild things, and in every season I had known it, it had been the home of a covey of bobwhite quail.

One winter's day of my first year on the Mason Farm, I had discovered Lone Field. And in early June of that year, I saw the first quail egg which, for me, was the beginning of the Lone Field covey. In the years that followed, I discovered that a new covey of quail was raised there each summer, sometimes by the same pair of the previous year, if they survived.

On the ground that June day, under foxtail grasses near a border of the field, I saw the single white egg, which I hoped would be followed by a full set of quail eggs. It was smaller than a domestic hen's and was the first of a dozen or more that a quail usually lays. It was top-shaped and lay in a grassy cradle under an arched roof of grasses. Had the brown quail been on her nest, I would never have seen the egg, nor would I have seen *her,* so perfectly does she blend with the living and dead plants she weaves about her. Without movement, sitting closely on the nest, she is hidden from the sharpest eyes of men, roving dogs, hawks, owls, and foxes.

ಜಿ During the laying period, the hen quail is away from her nest most of the time, and she visits it only once a day to add to it a single egg. It is a time of great danger for the exposed eggs. The eaters of quail eggs—foxes, raccoons, and opossums by night, and roving dogs, crows, and jays by day—are a constant threat to them. And a large blacksnake that I had seen sunning itself on the stones of the old homesite nearby would swallow every egg in the nest if it should discover them. But the exposure of her eggs was a risk that the five-ounce hen quail must take. It is her nature not to begin the long days and nights of incubation until she has laid her full set.

Even though the hen was not on the nest, I was sure that, with her rusty-brown mate, she was not far away. He attends her closely during this time and cannot seem to do enough for his slightly smaller companion. Following her about, he allows her to take the lead in their daily travels to their feeding places. In his devotion, he often tries to provide for her by running in a lively chase after a flying grasshopper. After catching it, he puffs himself up like a small rooster, holds the insect out stiffly in his bill, and calls to her in low clucking notes. She rushes to him, takes the crushed grasshopper, and eats it. He still provides for her in this way even when they are caring for their large brood of young.

From watching this same behavior in male birds of many kinds during the mating season, I am convinced that courtship feeding

—as it is called—renews and strengthens the bond between the mated pair. Unless one or the other of the adult quail is killed, their attachment for each other assures that the chicks will be guided and protected by both parents. Also, the extra food that the cock quail gives to his mate may strengthen her for the egg laying and her long vigil at the nest.

ᙓ I knew the pattern of this pair's courtship that now kept them from close association with others of their kind. It had started in spring of that first year while they were still running with the Lone Field covey that had grown from an original dozen to about twenty-five quail. The covey probably included not only this pair and some of their progeny of the previous summer, but other adults with survivors of their families, all of which had joined the Lone Field group that winter. And from my growing study of the quail, I learned that their strong attachment to the place came from its abundance of seeds, insects, and wild berries, and the protection from enemies and weather they found in the surrounding woods and thickets.

Early in April I had heard the first whistled *bob-white!* calls of the males, and one day I saw the first signs of pairing that precede the spring break-up of the covey. Driving slowly in my car over the narrow road that leads to Lone Field, I saw a group of two dozen quail feeding along the edge of the woods. I discovered that I could approach coveys closely, without frightening them, if I drove very slowly and made no quick motions inside the car. I stopped to watch.

The quail were running together, some picking at the floor of the woods as they fed. Others held their heads high and stood looking about nervously. There was an undercurrent of excitement in the covey as I heard their soft, conversational *kie-yew-week! kie-yew-week!* change to a rapid *kee-yew! kee-yew! kee-yew!* I began to see the reason for it.

Among the plain brown hens I saw half a dozen cocky little males. I could distinguish them from the females by the white stripe over each eye and the conspicuous white throat. They were running back and forth, no longer at peace with each other as they had been in the winter. With their feathers puffed out, they were paying much attention to the females; however, each time that two males met they stopped, faced each other, and lowered their heads threateningly. Sometimes they stood breast-to-breast and pecked at each other, then pecked at the ground as fighting roosters do. Once, two of them came together fiercely, and one finally vanquished the other by seizing it with his bill at the back of its neck and throwing his rival to the ground. All the while that they fought I heard them uttering a strange nasal sound, which is said to be the male's battle cry. The fight had lasted only about twenty seconds when one broke the other's hold and ran away. The victor followed him a short distance, then turned back to the covey.

While the fighting, bluffing, and chasing had been going on between the males, the females had run under the shelter of a thicket near the edge of the woods. Some of the males followed, and I heard excited calls, then saw the hens move out into the open again. They walked erectly with their tail feathers spread, their body feathers ruffled, and their wings slightly raised and quivering. The cock quail came with them and two of them suddenly began their courtship display, walking before the females and spreading their wings, with their heads lowered, showing the females their white head markings.

All the while that the males were bickering and displaying before the hens, I had been watching a cock quail and hen that had remained quietly together at the far side of the covey. Now they walked a little way in the direction of Lone Field. Both suddenly flew up quietly into the air and after a few quick wing-strokes, soared out of sight, deep into the woods. At that moment, something, perhaps a sound I did not hear, frightened the covey. With a roar of wings, which is their manner of noisy flight when they are startled, they flew away, darting around the trunks of trees in the gray woods until every brown bird had disappeared.

I could not be sure, of course, that the one pair in the covey which had flown first and appeared to have already been mated was the pair whose nest I found in June, but I have always believed that it was.

❧ I did not go near the quail's nest that June day after I discovered it with its single egg. I was afraid that if the hen should return and should see me, she might desert the nest. I had a plan that, if it worked, might tell me much about the pair and the success or failure of their nesting.

Either of the pair may build the nest, but often the male builds it with the hen looking on. He first digs a depression in the ground, which he excavates with his bill and claws. His mate stands quietly near him in the shade of grasses or weeds while he works. Occasionally she walks to the place to watch his progress as he scratches and digs in the soil. When he stops to rest, she steps into the hole to inspect it.

After the male has dug the depression to his satisfaction, he stands in it, reaches about with his bill, and pulls toward him the stems of weeds and grasses which he tucks into the hole. The pair are very sensitive to disturbance at this time. If anyone should stumble upon them while they are building the nest, they will abandon it and build a new one elsewhere.

Early the next morning, near the grassy edge of the cornfield, I dropped a four-sided, fitted-canvas cover, with canvas roof, over a light metal frame that I had set firmly in the ground. This was the blind I had often used to get close-up photographs of nesting birds. It was large enough that I could sit inside comfortably on a chair. And I could look out at eye level through peepholes in each of its four sides without being seen. I had watched sitting birds from the blind, often very close to their nests, without disturbing them, as long as I remained quiet.

But in this adventure, I was not interested in photography. I wanted to watch the behavior of the hen in and around the nest and to learn about her habits during the incubation of the eggs. If I were to be successful, I must keep silent—even the click of a camera shutter might frighten away the wary bird.

Inside the blind I settled myself with a notebook and pencil. I might have a long wait before the hen came to lay her second egg. And if anything had happened to her during the night, I might sit all day not knowing that she would never return. But it would be time that I was willing to spend freely, on the chance that I might watch her.

It was six o'clock in the morning. Outside the blind, I saw dew still sparkling on the grass. Quail do not usually travel far from their roosting places until the wet grasses have dried, but I did not want to miss seeing the hen if she should come to the nest early.

Far below, from the misty fields and flowering hedges of the Mason Farm, I heard the whistled *bob-white!* of unmated cock quail. Some of them, unable to acquire a mate, would give the *bob-white!* call all summer. This is a sign that they are bachelors, for only the unmated males continue this call throughout the nesting season. And the bachelors have fierce persistence in their desire for a family.

One summer, years before I met the Lone Field covey, I saw one of these bachelors try to attach himself to a quail family. Almost every day he took a beating from the cock quail that headed the group, because of his repeated attempts to join them. He often seemed dejected and his plumage disheveled from the attacks of the male. But always he was not far from the family that he wanted for his own.

Later, I saw him leading two chicks that were even younger than those of the family he wanted to join. Apparently many young quail, lost or separated from their families each summer, are adopted by these bachelors which tend the chicks as though they belonged to them. Eventually, when the defensive aggressiveness of the male that headed the family had subsided, the bachelor

was accepted, along with his two chicks, and became a member of
the covey.

◦◦ I pressed my nose to the canvas blind, my eyes close to the
peepholes that faced southeastward toward the nest in the grass.
Outside, the air was redolent with the odors of flowers and moist
earth. The sun was now an hour high, but at dawn it had been
only a blush, low in the east. Above it, a sickle moon and a planet
glowed high in the purple sky.

In the gloom, while crossing Morgan Creek on the way to Lone
Field, I had heard whippoorwills calling and had smelled the
sweetness of white-blooming elderberry thickets by the stream. At
the fields' edges the flowers of wild carrot and daisy fleabane shone
whitely in the pale light, and tall grasses bowed their tawny heads
loaded with purple seeds.

Outside the blind, a current of air swept from the pine woods
over Lone Field, bringing with it the fragrance of honeysuckle
thickets in flower. In the growing light, I began to watch alertly
for the small brown form of the hen quail hurrying back to her
nest.

I heard a joyous burst of robinlike caroling. It came from a
summer tanager that must have been in one of the giant oaks of
the old homesite at my back. Across the grass, in a thicket beyond
the quail's nest, an indigo bunting sang over and over a phrase
that sounded like *sweet-sweet, syrup, syrup, sweet!* Two crows
cawed loudly as they flew over my blind. Through the peepholes I
saw them swoop down over Lone Field, then disappear in the pine

woods to the south. They had apparently seen my structure and had uttered a warning, probably mounting higher in the air as they flew over, but they did not descend to the quail's nest. Its arched grasses, forming a roof, must have hidden the egg from the sharp-eyed crows.

Three hours passed. Lulled by the warmth of the day, I had almost fallen asleep when I heard the faint note of a quail. The sound came from the south, and not far away. Through a peephole I strained to look down Lone Field. Two small brown forms were running over the ground toward me. They stopped, looked about, and appeared to be listening. I could see that the nearer one was a hen quail with a male close behind her. As they stood at the edge of the field, I held my breath in an instinctive desire not to make a sound.

Again the hen started toward me, followed closely by the male. When she was opposite her nest, she stopped. She stood about ten feet from my lookout, holding her head high, her brown eyes bright in the morning sunshine. The male halted a few yards beyond her, standing very erect.

For the first time the hen seemed aware of my blind. She cocked her head sideways and looked sharply toward me. Fearful that she might feel the intensity of my gaze, I looked slightly away. For a few seconds the quail stood motionless. Then she ran through the grass to her nest. She stared down at the egg before she turned and settled on it, her face at the nest entrance and looking toward me. At the end of two minutes she rose slightly—I believe to expel her second egg—then settled on the nest again. She was quite relaxed and possibly relieved at laying the egg, which she cannot withhold after it reaches a certain development in her oviduct.

Five minutes passed. The hen got up and stepped out of her nest. I could see her second egg lying beside the first one. Her throat was pulsating in the heat as she stood looking around her. Then she ran to join the cock quail, which had been waiting for her at the exact spot where she had left him. They skulked a short distance through rows of green corn, then flew silently away toward Laurel Hill Woods. I stepped out of my blind to watch. Halfway across Lone Field they started to glide downward. I saw them alight at the border of the woods and run under a thicket.

For two weeks I stayed away from the nest. I knew that predators often find and eat the eggs of birds whose nests have been too much visited by photographers. Apparently, dogs, cats, and foxes sometimes follow their footsteps, possibly out of curiosity, and then find the birds' nests and eggs. I did not want to jeopardize these. Quail's nests are hard to find and my blind was in perfect position for observations of the hen.

A hen quail usually lays an egg a day until she reaches twelve, fourteen, or even fifteen. Then she may wait a day or two or a week before she starts her incubation; some hens will start incubating as soon as they have laid the last egg. And if a dog, fox, or other animal eats her eggs, and she escapes, she will go elsewhere to build a new nest and to lay a second set. If the second clutch is destroyed, she may lay a third, and will keep trying until she hatches a brood, even though it is in late summer or fall. The drive of a hen quail and her mate to raise a family is a marvel of tenacity and purpose.

I had pinned a sign to my blind: WILDLIFE PHOTOGRAPHER AT WORK. I hoped that it would keep away any curious person who might happen upon it and not understand its use. On the fourteenth day, when I returned, the blind was intact. Not a human footprint was near except my own, now almost washed away by a mid-June rain. Lone Field, remote and isolated, might not have any human visitors until the fall hunting season arrived.

As I approached the blind I did not glance toward the nest until after I was hidden inside. When I looked through the peepholes I saw the hen quail on her nest. She was sitting motionless, looking straight ahead. I had no way of knowing that I might have startled her, but I knew by her refusal to run or to fly that she must be incubating her eggs.

For twenty-three days after she had laid the last egg of her set, the hen sat closely on the nest, leaving it only once a day to feed. Her devotion to her eggs was touching. One rainy night I flashed my light at the tangle of grass to see if she were on the nest. She was there, with rain dripping from her back, but with her feathers spread to protect the eggs and to keep them warm.

Sometimes, during the day, I saw her napping, her eyes partly closed. But at the scream of a red-tailed hawk soaring over Laurel Hill, I saw her awaken with a start and sit very taut, as if she were about to spring into the air. Despite her apparent fear, she had little to dread from the redtails. Few of these big, clumsy birds can catch a healthy adult quail in its bulletlike flight, but once I had seen a hunting Cooper's hawk catch one on the wing.

The male stayed away while the hen was incubating, joining his mate each day at her call, but only when she was some distance from the nest. Whether by instinct or a dim reasoning, he chose not to come near. To do so might attract the attention of a natural enemy, which might then discover the nest.

After the hen found the cock quail, in response to his calls, they moved quickly away together. Once I saw them running along the field's edge, catching grasshoppers and picking up the small seeds of grasses and clovers. Sometimes they leaped into the air to snatch a blackberry from a bush.

I noticed that the length of time that the hen stayed off the nest, during incubation, depended on the weather. If it were wet and cool, her absences were usually of no more than an hour or two; if the day were hot and dry, she stayed away much longer, seeming to know that there was no danger of the eggs being chilled. One warm day, during one of the hen's long absences, I went swiftly and quietly to the nest to see how many eggs she had laid. There were fourteen.

On July 11, the twenty-third day of the hen's incubation and the hatching date for her eggs, I entered the blind at five o'clock in the morning. Some quail hatch their eggs in twenty-two days, but I took the chance that this one would hatch them in the usual time and that I might see the chicks. It was still too dark to see the nest through the early-morning gloom, but I had not long to wait. I had slit the peepholes sufficient that I could look through them with the aid of my powerful binocular and see every detail of the nest.

As the light increased, I saw the arched roof of the nest grasses and, finally, in the shadows, the hen quail herself. She was sitting on the nest facing me, and as the day brightened, I saw her rise slightly, look beneath her, then settle herself again, her feathers spread wide.

I was sure now by her behavior that the eggs had hatched, or were hatching, and that her concern was not for the eggs but for the chicks themselves. I knew the struggle that must be going on under the small brown hen. During the last forty-eight hours of her incubation, each of the fourteen chicks under her has been working hard within the egg. Almost desperately, it seems, each has pushed and turned, using the tiny projection, or egg tooth, on top of its bill to cut through the shell. As each chick pushed upward with its head against the inside circumference of the egg, it cracked a line almost completely around the larger, or top-shaped, end.

& 3 I once held a quail egg in my hands during the last minute of its hatching and beheld the miracle of emergence that I believed was now going on under the Lone Field hen: the peeping chick, pushing and heaving violently within, rolled the cracked egg about in my hand. Suddenly it kicked the shell open, which fell apart with only a small, hinged piece keeping the rounded top from separating completely from the lower part. And there, sprawled in my palm, was a chick very wet from its life inside the shell.

Within a minute the young quail sat up weakly and looked around. It tried to run, but when I cupped my hands around it, it crouched within the warmth of my palms, chirping contentedly. Within ten minutes its baby down had dried. I opened my hands part way to look at the bright-eyed bird. It was a puffy ball of chestnut down, with a black streak in back of each eye. It weighed not quite a quarter of an ounce.

❧ The July day had grown light enough that I could plainly see the hen quail on her nest and her every movement. She rose several times to look beneath her, and I heard for the first time the peeping of the chicks. Through my binocular I saw several small heads pop out of her feathers, then draw back into them again. The hen was holding the chicks in the nest by squatting over them, warming them and their wet natal down with her feathers and the heat from her body. Newly hatched quail may die of pneumonia if they are allowed to run about before they have dried.

Three hours later, I saw the hen step out of the nest surrounded by her dried and peeping chicks. I tried to count them as they ran about the parent, beating their tiny wings to keep their balance and tumbling over the smallest obstacles. To these fluttering bits of down, each no larger than a golf ball, a clod of earth was a mountain to be conquered; a patch of grass, a jungle to be struggled through. I thought there were fourteen, and later, when I counted the discarded eggshells in the empty nest, I knew that all had hatched.

But how could they survive, these chicks, soft as milkweed and thistledown? I had forgotten for the moment the parents—tough, wary, and resourceful, fearless and strong, ready to attack or to lure away the weasel, fox, or snake—and how obedient were the young, that scatter at the parents' warning, disappearing under a twig or a leaf until the danger has passed.

The hen wasted no time getting away, moving off through the grass and clucking softly to her following brood. Then I heard her whistle the bobwhite's rally call, known and loved by all country people. Soft it came, with a break in the middle: *Whirl-ah-hee! whirl-ah-hee!* It is the call that brings together the mated pair or the scattered members of the covey.

I heard the male answer and saw him hurry from the cornfield to join her. They were united now, the Lone Field covey, and they would stay together until the following spring.

Restless
Autumn

In September a change begins on the Mason Farm. An unease is there, and I see it and hear it in the life that in vast plenty spills over the land. The wild harvest is at its height, just before summer's end and the coming season of cold. Millions of the nectar gatherers—wild bees, wasps, and syrphus flies—hum at the purple-and-white flowers of the thickets of lespedezas, over whole fields of white-topped Eupatoriums, the gold and white of the roadside rabbit tobacco, the yellow blooms of the partridge pea, the moundlike flower clusters of Bidens that scent the air like new-mown hay. The goldenrods are still in blossom, and over their graceful sprays swarm legions of yellow soldier beetles seeking the rich flower pollen.

Millions, perhaps billions, of beetles, crickets, caterpillars, and grasshoppers run, jump, crawl, or fly through the brown weeds and grasses. Thousands of butterflies and day-flying moths, in black, browns, red, orange, blue, silver, white, yellow, and gold flutter over the fields in a ceaseless hunt for the nectar they find in every autumn wildflower.

Tawny grasses and weeds are loaded with seeds that the quail and a host of songbirds eat and that hordes of wild mice gather for their food stores. Some of these plants are still in flower in the dried ditches by the open fields: the yellow spikes of the tall Sorghastrum, or Indian grass, the purple, bottle-brush heads of a wild Panicum, the blue of Lobelia, the pink-red flowers and stems of smartweed— all shining in the soft September sunlight.

Walking silently in the dust of the roads at night, I hear
the rustle of raccoons stripping the yellow ears from the
brown stalks of corn at the woods' edge and the faint squeaks
of flying squirrels in Laurel Hill Woods. Now is the time,
early in September, when the chorus of insects, active
after dark, is a splendid orchestration of wing rubbed
against wing: the *chah-chah-chah!* of katydids, the silver-
bell sound of pale-green tree crickets, the tinkling of millions
of black ground crickets. And obliterating all other
sounds as I pass, there is the sharp, continuous
z-z-z-z-z-z-z-z-z! of a long-horned grasshopper perched on
a stem of roadside grass. I walk on as the buzz dies in
the distance, and the katydids and crickets again fill the night
for me with their sounds.

A sphinx moth passes like a winged bullet, and I see hundreds of small moths dancing over the road ahead in the
circle of my light. In the distance, from Big Oak Woods,
I hear the sweet, quavering whistle of a screech owl. Then
a brown whippoorwill flutters up from the road and flies
away into the outer dark, escaping my beam of light.

During the third week in September the fever of the wild
harvest is still upon the land. But with the continuing warm
days have come sharply cooler nights, and the wild
things show the beginning of another change. It comes
on a day, among days of shimmering beauty, when I see
the deepening red of the dogwood leaves and of sweet
gum and swamp maple against the green of pines, a day

of muted sounds and of a light haze over the fields when I am in a dreamlike world in which there is no passing of time. Then I read a new sign and I know that lovely September is nearing its end.

Walking along the old road, I stop and look toward the sun, westward across a field and toward the woods beyond. Suddenly I see, in the bright-yellow light, the glittering wings of thousands of dragonflies, the first I have seen this autumn in their migration. And on that day, I see some of the last of the chimney swifts—hundreds circling over the brown cornfields—snatching in flight at the insect hordes rising upward on the warm eddies of air. That night, under the cold, star-filled skies, I hear the sweet chirps of the first migrating birds, their voices in the dark like the piping of hylas in spring. The next day, in Big Oak Woods and in the green-gold trees along Morgan Creek, I see rose-breasted grosbeaks, thrushes, and a flood of brilliantly colored warblers that have arrived from the north. In a few days they are gone, and the swifts too, with the dragonflies that have left on the long trail to the south.

Out of September, October comes slowly with its warm, golden days but with nights of frost and the very last of the migrating birds. The yellow-breasted meadowlarks gather in flocks and feed over the corn and weed stubble, which they share with the gray mourning doves that winter there and with the black crows whirling like bits of charred paper over the brown fields. In the sunshine, blue jays fly in long files from woods to woods, moving southward; and on Muskrat Pond, passing teal, black ducks, and grebes splash down, feed for a few days, and are gone. A few chorus frogs still call *c-a-r-i-c-k!* *c-a-r-i-c-k!* from the roadside ditches. I hear a lone piping call of a spring peeper from Big Oak Woods.

By the middle of the month, most flowers, except the goldenrods are gone, but the late-blooming frost asters now whiten the fields and woods' edges. The cold nights have killed all but a few of the butterflies. Only the viceroy, the pearl crescent, the buckeye, the sleepy orange, and the little sulphur flutter weakly up and down the dusty roads where the trails of raccoons and opossums lead to persimmon thickets and wild-grape tangles.

Then, following a day in late October, when the small chinquapin nuts lie brown under the trees and the fleecy white clouds sail like ships in the sky, comes a change. One morning there is a downpouring of cold rain, and that afternoon winds sweep the Mason Farm, sending vast numbers of leaves whirling to the ground. Some of the larger ones fall with a rattle, others with a whisper or a sigh. It is the time of the animal harvest of acorns and nuts, and I prepare to go in the night to search again for flying squirrels.

CHAPTER X

Flying Squirrels: Phantoms of the Night

One summer, when I was a field naturalist working for the Federal Government, I lived in a boarding house in a small town in Western Pennsylvania. I had gone to my room at midnight and had been sleeping I knew not how long, when I felt something strike my bed. I stirred, half awake, half in a world of strange, violent dreams.

I opened my eyes. Moonlight from low in the western sky flooded through my window, but it was partly blotted out by a small, dark figure that sat squarely on my chest. Its short, slightly uptilted nose was close to mine, and its big luminous eyes stared at me from inches away. I saw a whiskered face and rounded ears. For the briefest moment I thought of elves and goblins, then I awakened.

This was no fantasy. The big-eyed creature on my chest was Hepsey, my four-ounce flying squirrel. She was leaning forward, peering into my face. Before I had left my room that evening I had forgotten to leave a food supply in her nest box.

I got up and walked to my bureau. From a drawer I took a tin box and reached for a hickory nut. As I got out of bed, Hepsey had leaped to the floor. She raced up a leg of my pajamas to my shoulders, the four claws of her front feet and the five on her hind ones digging into my skin. As I drew a nut out of the box, Hepsey was there to take it gently from my fingers. Then she leaped into the air. As the squirrel left my arm, she spread wide the soft, furry skin between her front feet and hind legs and glided swiftly away. With a flip of her tail that jerked her upright, she alighted flat against her small, square nest box, which I had fastened to a corner of my room. Then she whisked inside through the 1½-inch entrance hole.

Though Hepsey sometimes ate while sitting in my hands, the inside of the box was her favorite feeding place. It seemed to satisfy some need of hers for security while she was eating. Perhaps for the same reason she often crawled into one of my wide shirt pockets and slept while I sat quietly reading. It was a self-protective habit, an inherited racial one of Hepsey's that I was to remember when I began to study wild flying squirrels. And because her behavior in captivity was so much like that of her wild relatives, her story, inevitably, was woven into theirs.

ಇ That summer, Hepsey had come into my life when a Pennsylvania farmer I knew stopped me one day as I drove by his house. He held something small, cupped and hidden in his powerful hands. Did I want to raise a flying squirrel? The night before, a roaring wind had split an old oak in his yard and had tumbled a hollow limb and the nest within it to the ground. The mother flying squirrel and three of her young ones had been killed, but this one had survived. Because of her bright-eyed curiosity and because, from the start, she quickly became "hep" to her new world, I called her Hepsey.

The day that I got Hepsey she was well furred and strong enough to move about slowly. She was about seven or eight weeks old, and she ate slices of apple, carrots, lettuce, and bread, besides the milk I fed her with an eyedropper. When she crawled over my arms and shoulders, sniffing curiously at my shirt, she showed no fear. My landlady permitted me to keep Hepsey in my room, at least for a while, because of the young squirrel's helplessness and her dependence on me. Beau, her mate, came to me later, but in a very different way, and he sired Hepsey's first litter.

ε‍δ Usually a naturalist fails to study an animal not through lack of interest, but through lack of opportunity. Years after Hepsey, I knew little more about the behavior of flying squirrels than that which she, and later her mate, had taught me.

I had read about flying squirrels in a general way. There were two species: a northern flying squirrel that lived in woodlands across the northern United States and Canada, west to the Pacific and to Alaska and south into California and Utah; and the southern flying squirrel of the eastern states and the Middle West. The southern flying squirrel also lived over a vast area—from northern New England and southern Ontario south into Florida and west to parts of Texas, Oklahoma, Kansas, in most of Iowa, and in parts of Minnesota and Wisconsin.

The southern flying squirrel was slightly smaller than the

northern one. It was about eight to ten inches long, including its four-inch flattened tail. It was warm-buff and gray over its head, back, and tail, and its underparts were creamy white. This was the species to which Hepsey had belonged. And even though smaller than the northern flying squirrel, the southern one was said to be the more aggressive. Wherever their woodland ranges overlapped, the southern species usually displaced the northern one. I learned that the two were separated widely in their ranges by a physical fact not related to aggression at all. Because it is smaller and its body has a greater heat loss in winter, the southern flying squirrel cannot live as far north as its larger cousin.

During my first winter and summer on the Mason Farm, I thought it hopeless to try to study wild flying squirrels. They were too elusive, too difficult to see in the dark, too wary of lights for me to learn their secret ways. Besides being the only North American squirrels that were strictly nocturnal, they were the only native ones that "flew," or glided through the air. As soon as the white beam of my head lamp lighted them, I saw only a flash of ruby red from their eyes before they disappeared—their pale forms floating away under the crowns of the trees like phantoms in the night.

Beginning in the fall of my first year on the Mason Farm, I began to search intensively for flying squirrels. With the longer hours of darkness and the ripening of hickory nuts on Laurel Hill, I heard more and more of them moving about in the woods at night. And gradually I began to piece together a part of their story.

It began on a September evening, soft with starshine and the flutter of moths. As I walked in the faint light over the grassy road that led to the big hickory tree at the edge of Laurel Hill Woods, the twitter of thousands of tree crickets silvered the dusk with sound. Above the purr of the crickets came the harsh *scratch-it! scratch-it!* of green katydids in the trees. A whippoorwill flew up from the road at my feet, all brown in the glare of my head lamp, which I had switched on at the moment of the bird's quick flight.

At the tall hickory I stopped in the gloom and spread a blanket on the sand of the old road. Then I lay down to listen. The tree bore a heavy crop of hickory nuts, still hanging in green-hulled pairs at the ends of the twigs and branches. That day I had seen gray squirrels gathering them, and I had hoped that flying squirrels might visit the tree that night. Hepsey had preferred hickory nuts to all other food I had offered her, and I was sure that wild flying squirrels shared her tastes. In the days ahead, in my studies of the food stores of flying squirrels on Laurel Hill, I was to discover that they did prefer hickory nuts, even to the sweet acorns of the white oak trees.

I had been lying flat in silence for fifteen minutes. It was almost dark when I heard a faint *p-s-s-s-e-e-e-k!* and a thump as if some animal had struck the trunk of the hickory. It was too dark to see, but I heard other sharp chirps which I recognized as the conversational calls such as Hepsey had often given in the dark. Then I heard a rustling in the branches of the tree and a rattle as some object fell through the branches to the ground.

I flashed my spotlight on the outermost branch from which the sound had come. In the glare I saw a flying squirrel huddled on a branch with what appeared to be a partly hulled hickory nut in its mouth. Then it was gone, and the small rustling sounds ceased as quickly as they had begun.

My light must have frightened away every flying squirrel in the tree. From the sounds I had heard as they cut off the hickory nuts I was sure that there must have been at least half a dozen of them working in the dusk. Later, I heard them again, but as the orange moon rose behind Big Oak Woods they fell silent. A barred owl hooted, and I lay watching the glorious night.

I fell asleep for a while but kept my vigil most of the time. At midnight the full moon shone so brightly that I could see bats darting about like small ghosts in the air overhead. By their quick turns I was sure that they were feeding upon the fluttering moths that filled the night.

There were no more sounds of flying squirrels until just before dawn. The moon was low in the west when I heard a few more chirps and rustlings in the tree. But with the first faint light in the east, the sounds ceased.

⁊ That fall and winter I learned that flying squirrels did not often come out on moonlit nights or when it rained or when the wind blew hard. Perhaps their aversion to moonlight helped many of them to escape the pair of great horned owls that hooted and moaned from the ridge top of Laurel Hill and the barred owls that *hoo-ah*'d from the depths of Siler's Bog. And when it rained or the wind blew, the patter and rush of falling drops and the rustle of leaves and creaking limbs might hide the sounds of stalking foxes.

But on dark nights, either clear or overcast, as fall and early winter came to Laurel Hill, the flying squirrels were out during three periods of time: shortly after dusk, around midnight, and just before dawn.

This was the rhythm of night activity that Hepsey had followed. Often she had awakened me as she scampered about my room late at night or early in the morning. Hers was a built-in rhythm over each twenty-four hours, inherited from her wild ancestors, an adaptation to the world of darkness that must have been millions of years old.

Bright lights make a flying squirrel uncomfortable, perhaps both physically and psychologically. Most animals of the night, like Hepsey, have large eyes that are dark-adapted. I noticed that she avoided strong light and came out only in the dimness of twilight or in the soft glow of a blue light bulb that I put in my lamp for her dusk-time or late-at-night play. When it was still light, before I went to dinner, I often lifted her out of her box while she was still full of sleep and scratched behind her ears or along her cheeks and chin. When she was awake she ran up my arms to my shoulders and then to my head to groom my hair as one animal grooms another's fur. Sometimes she sat on my shoulders and nipped gently at one of my ears or sniffed inside it rapidly and noisily. I seemed a constant source of investigation for her. I was her only companion, and I must have satisfied her need for the attention she might have given another squirrel.

There was only one thing about my behavior that terrified Hepsey. If I rattled a paper on my desk or rustled the newspaper I was reading, she dashed up the bureau or any other object from which she could glide to her nest box. I think the dry whisper of the papers suggested the rustling of leaves—a sound of danger to most small wild animals.

ᐤᢓ On Laurel Hill, as the nights grew longer and autumn lengthened into winter, the flying squirrels seemed in a frenzy to collect the ripening hickory nuts and acorns. They were more and more active and sometimes worked all night, sifting through the brown leaves under the trees with their noses and busy forepaws. In the dark they often uttered low chucks that Hepsey had given when she was contented or pleased, or sharp notes and squeals that expressed their displeasure. If they were frightened, they barked, high-pitched but soft, and not nearly so loud as a gray squirrel. One autumn night I heard a small, terrified cry, which was followed by a long silence. I think an owl, a fox, or perhaps a raccoon had caught one of the flying squirrels.

ᐤᢓ That autumn and winter, on sunny days, I climbed the gray-trunked oak and hickory slopes of Laurel Hill searching for the homes of flying squirrels. Through the densely covered floor of brown leaves I shuffled, stumbling over concealed rocks and sometimes falling as I plunged to my knees in hidden, rotted-out stump holes.

Upward I followed the course of Yancey Brook, with its small pools of black water and the welcome green of Christmas ferns and wild ginger peeping from the fallen leaves along its banks. Ranging away from the brook, I rapped on every hollow tree. Of the dozens I struck, flying squirrels came leaping out of woodpecker holes near the tops of ten dead trees. Some came out singly; others in groups of six to eight. Those in groups had gathered together for warmth against the winter cold. Most of the entrance holes to their dens were ten to twenty feet from the ground. I found I could easily reach them with a light extension ladder.

One curious fact I discovered about the den-trees of these squirrels—all were within fifty to two hundred feet of the brook. Later, a student of flying squirrels who had kept many of them in captivity told me that his squirrels could not live more than two days without water. I had kept Hepsey provided with a small dish of water at all times and had never questioned her need for it. But the student's experience told me why these dens in the wild were in trees from which a flying squirrel could frequently glide to water without the risk of traveling long distances for it.

Hepsey taught me another lesson about the capabilities of the wild flying squirrels of Laurel Hill. In an experiment, I put one hundred hickory nuts on my bureau at dusk one fall evening to see what she would do with them. By midnight, when I returned to my room, she had stored them all. Some were in her nest box, others were in the folds of the window drapes, some were in my shoes under the bed, and others in the pockets of my shirt and trousers that hung outside my closet door. Just as the wild flying squirrels of Laurel Hill have food storage places in holes in trees a short distance from the home nest, or in the forks of limbs and under fallen leaves of the forest floor, these had been Hepsey's hiding places for her stores.

At midnight when I came to my room, Hepsey had disappeared. I did not look for her but counted another one hundred hickory nuts and spread them on my bureau. The next morning when I got up, every nut was gone. Hepsey had picked up and stored two hundred in one night.

When I began to study the nut gathering of flying squirrels on Laurel Hill, I made a quick calculation. Knowing Hepsey's ability, I was sure that each wild squirrel, during a good crop year of hickory nuts, could also store at least two hundred in one night, and could probably do so within a few hours. I had noted that the flying squirrels began their nut gathering in September and October, and that it reached its height in November. It ended in January, with the sharpest winter cold and the snow that sifted down over the wooded slopes.

Considering only those nights when I was certain that flying squirrels would be gathering nuts or acorns on Laurel Hill and the number I found in some of their stores, I believe that each could have harvested ten to twelve thousand in a season. Each probably gathered far less. And from uneaten flying squirrel caches I found in the hollows of trees, and later in bird nesting boxes, I was sure that they usually stored many more than they ate. Hepsey seldom ate more than one or two hickory nuts in a night, although a more active wild flying squirrel might eat more.

After Hepsey had stored a hickory nut or acorn, she would not store that same nut again. Her sense of smell or taste was so keen that she distinguished at once a nut she had had in her mouth before and refused to carry it away. With this ability, a flying squirrel would not waste energy picking up and restoring the same foods.

⟡ With the coming of February and the green of newly leafed honeysuckle thickets on Laurel Hill, I saw the beginning of the break-up of the groups of flying squirrels that had huddled together in the hollows of trees all winter. Piled one upon another, they had slept through cold and storms. Each squirrel had warmed its companions, and their accumulated body heat had built a microclimate of comfort within that had protected them from the cold.

With the warming sun of February and March, those female flying squirrels that had mated while huddled with the males in the winter dens started the dispersal. They left the groups and moved into hollows by themselves. There, late in their forty-day pregnancies, they built nests of finely shredded cedar bark that they had stripped from trees on Laurel Hill. Some of their nesting hollows held a quart of bark woven into a ball. One that I found within the abandoned home of a woodpecker was built of fine strips of the golden inner bark from a honeysuckle vine. These were the nurseries for the young.

⟡ I had learned from Hepsey, and from wild flying squirrels that I caught in their dens on Laurel Hill, that a female has four pairs of breasts along the sides of her belly between the front feet and hind legs. She is capable of nursing eight young, but her usual number is from two to six. She usually has two litters a year—one born in late winter or spring, the other in July or August or sometimes later in the fall.

For a week before the female gives birth, she drives away from her nest-tree any adult flying squirrel, especially a male. Of all squirrels, flying squirrels are the most fond of meat and will eat the eggs or young of small birds if they happen upon a nest. And they will eat young mice and shrews if they find them. I am sure that the female flying squirrels chase away the males because they sense their carnivorous appetites.

From my experience with Hepsey, I knew that she had kept Beau, her mate, away from her young ones until they were at least sixty days old. At that age, the young squirrels are large enough that an adult male will not mistake them for young mice to be eaten, and he will accept them as his own.

Beau, a wild flying squirrel, came to me one summer, many years ago, at the time I had Hepsey. One June day I was working in a Pennsylvania woodland, helping some foresters make a timber survey of the plot. An eight-foot-tall dead chestnut stub blocked our compass line. As I pushed it to the ground, two flying squirrels leaped in succession from the hollow top and glided toward the base of a nearby tree. The first to leave the hollow escaped by running up the trunk and disappearing among the green leaves of this forest giant. I was too occupied with the second one to know where the first one had gone. I had wanted a mate for Hepsey, and the second flying squirrel I saw leaving the stub might be a male. By the time it alighted at the bottom of the same tree, I was there to catch it in my hands.

Because I squeezed its body slightly to keep it from wriggling from my grasp, the squirrel turned its head and bit my hands. But I kept my hold on the small, furry creature until one of the foresters offered me his wide-brimmed, deep-crowned hat. I pushed the squirrel inside, folded the rim of the hat over my prize, and took it home.

Later, I examined it while wearing heavy gloves, but this time it did not try to bite. I remember that I was excited when I discovered that it was a fine male. He was in breeding condition, too, because his testes were descended into his scrotum. I named him Beau, wondering all the while if Hepsey would accept him.

Long before I caught Beau, I had transferred Hepsey to a large outdoor cage. Each day she slept in the darkness of the nest box, which I had wired to the inside of the enclosure. She came out only at dusk or at night to feed and to glide or run about. I kept up our companionship by often standing in the cage in the dark while she ran up my trousers and then into my pockets for the hickory nuts, acorns, or sunflower seeds that I had put there. Sometimes I caught her in my hands and gently stroked her sides and back. When she had had enough, she would nip one of my fingers lightly, slip out of my hands, and glide away.

When I released Beau in Hepsey's cage, he leaped from my hands and soared to the far side of the pen. He ran up one of the eight-foot-high sides and clung motionless to the wire. I closed the gate quietly and walked away. Two hours later, when I returned, Beau had disappeared. From Hepsey's nest box I heard a low, birdlike chirp, then silence.

⁂ Hepsey and Beau had one habit that I never quite understood. At dusk I often sat with them in the outdoor cage to watch their behavior. As they moved about, whenever they met, they stopped to run their paws swiftly over each other. Then they brought their faces together and kissed much as prairie dogs do upon meeting. I was not sure of its significance, but this small ritual seemed a way of recognition between them. It was as though the two squirrels did not quite trust their eyesight and depended upon physical contact, and perhaps their sense of smell, to certainly identify each other.

⁂ Hepsey's three young were born near the end of July. I discovered them early one morning not long after their birth. I had looked in the box to check on Hepsey's welfare. She was crouched over the young squirrels while they nursed.

Gently I raised her until I could see the newborn babies in the nest hollow. They were hairless and pink. Their eyes were closed. Each was little more than two inches long. I could clearly see the fold of skin along each of their sides. Called the patagia, these were transparent, but later, when furred, they would be the functional "sails" on which each squirrel would glide about.

The young ones squeaked faintly as I drew one out of the nest box. When I put it on a sensitive balance, it weighed not quite a fifth of an ounce. At that moment Hepsey ran up my trousers to my hands, gripped the young squirrel in her mouth, and carried it inside the box. I closed the lid and left.

Hepsey spent most of her time with her family. She left them only a little while each day, early in the morning, or in the evening when she came out of the nest to feed. I had attached another box to a far corner of the pen. There Beau spent most of his time. If I caught him and carried him near Hepsey's box, he grew uneasy, and when I released him he hastened back to his corner of the enclosure. Two weeks before she had given birth, Hepsey had driven Beau away and he seemed to remember that he was not welcome near her nest.

I looked in at Hepsey each day. When her three young ones were 15 days old, I could see the first hair on their heads and along their backs, but other parts of their bodies were still naked. At 21 days, the young squirrels were covered with hairy down; at 28 days they opened their eyes for the first time.

When the youngsters were 30 days old, I tested Hepsey's protective maternal instinct. I took the young squirrels out of the box and put them on the ground. She instantly glided to them, picked one up, and washed it with her tongue. Then she grasped it by its belly fur with her teeth, climbed the wire, and took it inside the box. She returned for the other two and carried them back to the nest in the same way.

I learned that the maternal instinct of a flying squirrel is so strong that she will carry any young squirrels back to the nest box, whether they are hers or not. A friend of mine studied flying squirrels in captivity for many years. He has kept up to thirty in captivity for his detailed scientific studies. He told me that one mother that he tested retrieved thirty-five young squirrels and carried them into her nest box, although only four of them were her own. However, after her own young squirrels were 40 days old she rejected and even attacked other young squirrels that the experimenters offered her.

Apparently some change takes place in a female flying squirrel at that time, after which her devotion is to her own family and not to another.

When Hepsey's young were 53 days old, they were still nursing, but at 60 days they began to eat solid food. Gradually they ate corn, the bark of willow twigs and wild cherry, and acorns that I always kept in the pen for Hepsey and Beau. At 68 days, for the first time, I saw Beau approach one of the young squirrels and touch noses with it. Hepsey made no move toward him, and I knew that Beau had been accepted by his family. The young squirrels were very playful now, chasing each other about the cage and calling shrilly, much like their parents. They even quarreled among themselves over food. Often, when Hepsey was eating a hickory nut, they tried to take it from her. She scolded and pushed them away with her forepaws, but when they persisted, she gave up the nut. When all of the youngsters were finally eating, she went to a corner of the cage and ate undisturbed.

By fall, Hepsey's young were almost as large as she. In September of that year, the government notified me that I was to be transferred to another state. I did not want to give up the squirrels, especially Hepsey and Beau. To turn Hepsey and her youngsters loose in the nearest woods might have sentenced them to instant death. They were innocent of the world of hawks, owls, and foxes. Only Beau was likely to survive. He had been a wild squirrel at one time, conditioned to the danger of the owl's soft flight, the constant threat of rending teeth and talons. But to take Beau away from Hepsey did not seem right.

When I got into my loaded car to drive the four hundred miles to my new government station in upstate New York, Hepsey and Beau were in their nest box by my side. I had given away their youngsters to warmhearted friends of mine who loved the young squirrels. And at my new boarding house, my kindly landlady allowed me to build a large wire cage in her yard for Hepsey and Beau. There they had more litters of young, and each year, when they were weaned and on their own, I gave the young ones away.

Beau was at least eight years old when I found him one morning lying quietly in his box. Apparently he had died in his sleep. Hepsey, almost blind and feeble, died in my hands when she was ten. Both had lived about the longest lives possible for a flying squirrel, and both had died of old age.

The Webs
of November

Each year dies slowly and gracefully on the Mason Farm—not with paroxysms or wild contortions, but gently and imperceptibly, just as leaves fall day by day until the woods at last stand bare. Snow is rare in November and December, although frost often whitens the roads and corn-stubble fields and the dead weeds and grass. The skies are deeply blue, the balmy air smoky with the mist of Indian summer days, the fields brown, the woods golden, the rose hedges still green. Patches of scarlet and yellow leaves cling to some of the trees, giving lovely light and color to all the land.

The cold-blooded animals that must hibernate to survive are gone: the copperheads, black racers, king snakes, milk snakes, the secretive mole snakes, and the puff adder; the painted, and snapping, turtles and fence lizards; the frogs, toads, and salamanders. All have found places under the ground or in the mud where they will sleep until touched again by the warmth of spring.

When I walk over the farm in November, I see the delicate crane flies float out of the fields and drift away, many of them copulating in flight. Clouds of midges dance up and down in their aerial courtships, and I see, trailing across the road ahead, thousands of strands of spiders' silk glistening in the light of the winter sun. These are the webs of November, the bridges of young spiders that cast their slender lines on the wind and are carried away to start their lives in another, more distant place.

In Big Oak Woods, I see bluebirds and flocks of cedar waxwings, Carolina wrens, nuthatches, titmice, and chickadees. These are the year-round birds, more prominent since the songsters of summer—the tanagers, buntings, whippoorwills, robins, wood thrushes, thrashers, catbirds, and vireos—are gone.

Now the thickets, the weed-grown fields, and hedges rustle with the ground scratching of white-throated sparrows and juncos from the North, with towhees, cardinals, and song sparrows, all hunting ripe seeds and insects numbed by the early-winter cold.

In Finley Tract, I hear the mewing cries of yellow-bellied sapsuckers and the spirited singing of ruby-crowned kinglets that have come to these woods from the North. And on still days comes the light bill-tapping of woodpeckers in the forests, digging hollows in dead trees where they will be warm and dry and safe from owls through the long winter nights. Mockingbirds sing softly from the hedges where they nested in summer, and loggerhead shrikes rest for a while in the rose canes before moving farther south.

I remember, especially, a clear bright afternoon in December of my first year on the Mason Farm. I had walked eastward along a road north of Morgan Creek. It was a still day on which the slightest sounds traveled far: the light scratching of juncos, whitethroats, and a brown thrasher by a pine woods; the scurrying of mice in the grass; the cawing of crows a mile to the south.

The sunlight lay warm on a brown field north of the creek and glistened from the dead stalks of roadside weeds and grasses. When I reached Willow Oak Swamp, the wet fallen leaves muffled the sounds of my booted feet. I stopped. In the silence of the darkening woods, I heard not a twig snap, not the slightest rustle of a moving thing. It was as though the animals that lived there were motionless and waiting. Then, not far away, I heard the wild, sweet singing of a fox sparrow that had come from the North to winter in the thickets at the swamp's edge.

I moved on, stopping sometimes in the purple shadows to listen and to look up at the rays of afternoon light touching the tops of the trees. Suddenly I heard, close by, the plaintive yelp of a wild turkey: *K-e-o-w-k, k-e-o-w-k, k-e-o-w-k, k-e-o-w-k!* Then, silence. When I searched the woods ahead, the turkey had gone. It was the first one I had heard on the Mason Farm, but it was not to be the last.

CHAPTER XI

The Black Gobbler of Willow Oak Swamp

ॐ The big gobbler had become a legend long before I saw him. Black as a crow, and with his small blue head raised to its full four-foot height above the ground, he was the most magnificent wild animal—furred or feathered—I have ever seen. There is something noble and touching in the pride of a wild thing. I saw it in the black gobbler, in his aloneness and in his defiance, mixed with an uncanny keenness of eyes and ears that made even those who hunted him look upon him with awe. There was mystery about him, too. Perhaps it lay in his strange disappearances and his wild cunning that made him invulnerable for years to even the smartest turkey hunters.

It was the ability of the black gobbler to escape traps, dogs, men and their guns, horned owls, foxes, and bobcats that put me on his side. I searched for him, not as a hunter, but as one who wanted to be assured that a hero was not slain; that Mercury still had his winged feet and the power of his great black sails which, in minutes, could put a whole North Carolina valley between him and his pursuers.

From hunters who knew the black gobbler before I did, I learned that he was one of a brood of ten that had hatched one spring day on the Mason Farm. Someone had stumbled on the hen and her nest under a greenbrier thicket. The nest was a leaf-lined depression in the ground. The chicks had just hatched and were not yet dry. The hen flew angrily at the head of the man who had disturbed her brood, but before he turned away from her attack, he saw that one of the downy, pale-brown chicks was jet black.

Much about the black gobbler's early life had to be conjectured, because no one saw him until the following spring. Hunters and naturalists know that young male turkeys in their first summer stay with the adult hens and young females, which make up about half of each brood. It was probable that the black gobbler got his early training from his mother and first learned to catch insects, a main food of young turkeys, by following her example. She catches insects in her bill, then clucks to the chicks, which run to her. If the insect is too large for the young turkeys to swallow, with her bill she breaks it up on the ground into small pieces, then feeds it to them.

By December, young males separate from the hens, which, with the young females, remain together as a flock throughout the winter. Now the young gobblers of the year travel together and are eating—besides insects—acorns, dogwood berries, and the seeds of pine trees.

No one saw the young black gobbler during his first winter, but in spring, long after the hunting season was over, a hunter reported that he had seen him go to roost at dusk in Willow Oak Swamp. He had flown up into a tree with three other first-year gobblers that may have been his brothers.

ℰℰ Not until they are two or three years old are the younger males permitted to join with the four- or five-year-old gobblers. These older turkeys are the patriarchs that do most of the breeding, and they dominate the wild flocks. A one- or two-year-old gobbler may be capable of mating during his first or second spring, but he is usually prevented from doing so by the aggressiveness of the older males.

ℰℰ The black gobbler was a year and a few months old when, as a full-grown bird, he experienced his first hunting season. Even though a wild turkey does not reach his greatest weight of fourteen to seventeen pounds or more until he is at least two years old, the black gobbler was sought from the beginning. From the opening date of the wild turkey season in late November to its end in February he somehow escaped the daily barrage of gunfire. The great hunt for him was on.

A glossy, coppery-feathered wild gobbler is a prize, but a black one is so rare that few have ever been seen, and these were thought to have had an infusion of dark heredity from domestic black turkeys. But no domestic turkey, with its lack of wild alertness and inbred partial tameness, could have survived as had the black gobbler of Willow Oak Swamp. From the beginning, after having been shot at, he demonstrated why a wild turkey is the most difficult of all birds to kill. From his ancestors he had inherited wildness; while still young he had been made sharply aware of the dangers of his swamp and upland home by the parent hen turkey; and he must have learned how to escape foxes and horned owls through his own experiences and those of the wild gobblers that made up the male flocks.

I learned one day, from his four-inch track in the snow, that the black gobbler never walked near a thicket until he had circled it to avoid the possible rush of a hiding fox, and that he never stepped over a log large enough to conceal a bobcat before stopping to reconnoiter it. I also discovered that one of the black gobbler's favorite roosting trees was in the over-water branches of a syca-more on a bank of Morgan Creek in Willow Oak Swamp. Horned owls have been known to crowd a turkey from its roost at night. Then they strike it in the air with their talons and ride it to the ground, but they are thought to be afraid to do so when the roost is over water. And once the hunters got on the black gobbler's trail, he had become even wilder than his alert companions, be-cause, of them all, he was the most hunted. Some of my knowledge of his life habits I got from men who knew the bird well. But no one knew him as Rufus Blackwater did, and it was he and I who followed the gobbler to the strange conclusion of his story.

◆ A year and a few months after I had come to Chapel Hill, on a day in mid-May, I first saw the black gobbler. At the time, he was about seven years old, according to Rufus. At 4:30, during an early-morning walk on the Mason Farm, I heard a pair of barred owls calling from Willow Oak Swamp. While the light was still dim, I hid inside the leafy border of Big Oak Woods. The owls were calling in the swamp, beyond an old field, and I wanted to see if I could lure them closer.

I cupped my hands to my mouth and boomed their guttural cry, to which I got a quick answer from one of the owls. Then, from the dark of the swamp, I heard a wild turkey call: *Gil-obble-ob-ble-obble!* The sound was resonant and deep and came, I was sure, from an old gobbler. Apparently he was still on his roost.

Male turkeys will sometimes gobble in reply to any loud, sharp sound: the bark of a dog, the crash of a falling tree, a burst of laughter from campers. A game warden in Pennsylvania told me that a flock of wild turkeys came to his parked car, attracted by the music of his radio. In spring, males may be stimulated to gobble by the roar of a tractor, the buzz of a chain saw, or the clapping of one's hands. In Mississippi, wild turkeys have been known to gobble at the bawling of a calf or the drumming of a woodpecker. One old male in Pennsylvania paid no attention to these sounds, but gobbled whenever a jet plane flew over. Sounds that make turkeys gobble are of frequencies between two hundred and six thousand cycles per second.

This behavior seems to belie the bird's wild caution, for the gobble may give away the location of the turkey to the stalking hunter. I learned that this paradox of turkey nature, coupled with its strong curiosity, may have caused the deaths of many of the big males. One old hunter in South Carolina lured them within shooting range by waving a red handkerchief above his place of concealment and then slapping his hat against the sides of his boots to simulate the sounds of fighting gobblers.

◈ Crouched in my hiding place beside Big Oak Woods, I heard no more sounds from the owls. I remained silent because I did not want to risk frightening the gobbler by again imitating the owls' cries. A whippoorwill called, then was quiet. It may have gone to sleep, for, like an owl, it is a bird of the night. From the fields came the first dawn songs of indigo buntings and yellow-breasted chats. High in an oak, a blackpoll warbler lisped its first notes of the day.

At six o'clock, the sun sent long yellow rays across the field. Three dark forms moved slowly out of the swamp, and with sudden excitement I realized that they were wild turkeys. They were feeding at the field's edge, with their heads down, clipping with their bills the tender green tips of weeds and grasses. One suddenly ran ahead of the others in an awkward chase after a flying grasshopper.

Then, beyond the three, I saw another, darker form. Slowly, warily, it came out of the swamp. When it was fully out of the woods,

I saw its small periscopelike head raised high. Below the bare blue skin of its head and the red wattles of its throat, its slender, glossy, black-feathered neck widened to a massive black chest. Almost hidden in the grass, I saw the tops of its long reddish legs. They were graceful and strong like those of a race horse. Hanging from the middle of its broad chest, I saw a bundle of dark bristles fully twelve inches long; this was the beard of an old gobbler. But what impressed me most about this bird, other than his great size, was the rich sepia of his feathers. My hands, holding the binocular, trembled. I knew, at last, that I was looking at the black gobbler of Willow Oak Swamp.

The wild caution of the big gobbler contrasted sharply with the behavior of the three turkeys ahead of him. He moved slowly out into the field, step by step, turning his small head quickly to look in all directions; they fed quietly and unconcernedly, their dark backs humped high, their long necks and small heads pointing downward as they fed. Perhaps they had learned to rely on the wary old gobbler for their protection.

After he seemed assured that all was well, the gobbler lowered his head and slowly followed his companions. As the three moved farther into the field, I saw that two were the smaller, browner hens, without the gobbler beard, although some hens may have one. The other was a large gobbler—not as big or as black as the gobbler of Willow Oak Swamp—with a bristly beard that hung about eight inches below his broad chest.

The black gobbler hastened his pace and when he caught up with the three, he suddenly turned and ran a few steps toward one of the hens. Watching him through my binocular, and not daring to move, I had been fascinated by the beauty and wildness of the big bird. I was not prepared for his display. It came like a quick opening of a flower or the unfurling of a flag.

Within five feet of the hen, he suddenly lowered his wing tips to the ground and raised his broad black tail, which he spread like a fan. As swiftly as he had raised and opened his tail feathers, he had drawn his neck back until his head, now red with the blood of his emotions, rested between his shoulder feathers. With his breast, back, and belly feathers puffed straight out, he filled his body with air. Blown up to the full capacity of his skin, he looked like a big black ball. He ran a few steps toward the hen, his wings rasping as he dragged their tips over the ground. His spread tail was turned forward for her full view. Suddenly, he thrust out his chest. I heard a faint *puff,* a sharp *cluck,* then a booming sound as he forced the air out of his body. This is the male display that induces a hen, ready for copulation, to crouch before him on the ground. I did not see the act to its completion.

I had been leaning forward slightly, peering through the border thickets of Big Oak Woods. I was well concealed from the sharp-eyed turkeys, but before the hen could prostrate herself I straightened from my cramped position. At that moment a crow, which I had not seen approaching from the rear, flew over my head. It cawed sharply and the turkeys ran as swiftly as deer into Willow Oak Swamp. Careful as I had been, I had not reckoned on the watchfulness of a bird whose warning cries are heeded by almost all wild things.

I was disappointed that I had not seen the mating to its completion, but I *had* watched the unforgettable display. For a long

while, as I walked the two miles to my parked car, my heart
pounded with the excitement of what I had seen.

A month after I had seen for the first time the black gobbler, I met
Rufus Blackwater. In a small grocery store at the edge of town I
listened to him talk about wild turkeys. He was an avid hunter,
and in my sympathy for the black gobbler, I had to control
showing my anger at the slim little man as he told a group of
farmers of the gobblers he had shot. But he had never gotten the
black one, although he probably knew more about it than anyone
in the county.

The man unquestionably knew wild turkeys and their ways, and
in particular, he knew the black gobbler. I could learn much about
turkeys by becoming his friend. And I might even persuade Rufus
not to kill the black gobbler.

When I told Rufus of my experience in watching the courtship
strut of the much-hunted gobbler, without telling the place, the
dark eyes in his leatherlike face brightened.

"You've got to be a good woodsman or plain lucky to see *him!*"
he said. His tone was admiring, and I knew then that we might
become friends.

"There's a lot of turkey hunters around here," he said confid-
ingly, "and I think everyone of 'em has had a shot at the black
gobbler at one time, in season or out. And if he was to be killed,
you'd probably find his skin full of lead because his feathers are so
thick they'd turn the force of the shot, unless he was fired at real
close. Only a head shot'll kill a turkey outright," he said, "other-
wise you're liable to cripple or wound him.

"Hunters tried every way to kill the black gobbler. They've hunted him with dogs, and dogs are known to scare a turkey so bad he'll either fly right up into a tree, and when the hunters come up, get shot, or he'll hide in a thicket and when the dogs roust him, the hunters nail him. But they never came up on the black gobbler that way. When he got to runnin' ahead of the dogs, he'd run only far enough to put some trees and brush between him and the hunters, then he'd take off and fly a mile away to another part of his range.

"One fella tried to bait him with a trail of corn that he spread in the woods right up to a circle of traps. That's illegal, you know. The gobbler ate the corn, and when one of the traps snapped, he was so quick he jumped in the air and got caught only by the tip of the toe. The trap pinched it off and he got away. Nobody's ever lured him to a trap since.

"They've even hunted him at night after seein' him go to roost just before dark. Then they'd shine a light up into the tree and everybody'd fire at anything they'd see that looked like a roostin' turkey. But the black one always got away. They'd hear him beatin' his wings against the leaves and branches and he'd fly off so fast no one ever got a good shot at him. Sometimes," Rufus said, "I don't think anybody'll ever kill him. I'm the only one that hunts him now—others gave up long ago."

"Why don't you give him up?" I asked.

Rufus looked pained.

"I can't," he said.

"Why not?"

"Because I know he's there." He puffed on his cigarette. "I could give up smokin' a lot easier," he said.

🦃 At noon one October day, five months after I had seen the black gobbler's splendid courtship display, I saw him for the second time. I was turning a bend in the road that circles Big Oak Woods, when across a wide field at the edge of Finley Tract I saw a flutter of large black wings in a tree. Swiftly I brought my binocular to my eyes. Three wild turkeys were perched beside a grapevine that grew over the broken stub of a sweet gum. They were balancing awkwardly on the tree's branches, reaching out to pluck ripe grapes from the vine. All were gobblers and one of them was the black one of Willow Oak Swamp! Below them, in the field's edge, I saw a small cloud of dust rise from a fourth turkey that lay on its side, kicking dirt over its back as it took a dust bath.

Although I had stopped abruptly, six hundred feet away, and was rigidly still, the turkeys saw me as quickly as I had seen them. The big gobbler flew to the ground and the others followed. The one that had been taking a dust bath sprang to his feet, and all of them ran rapidly into the woods.

That was the last time that I saw the black gobbler in company with other turkeys. After the hunting season of that fall and winter, Rufus told me that three large gobblers had been killed several miles to the south on Edwards Mountain. He thought they were the three that I had seen with the black gobbler that October day, but the black one was not among them. He had survived his eighth hunting season and was wilder and warier than ever. He had become a hermit gobbler—one that lives alone, is the oldest turkey on the range, is usually of extraordinary size, and is the only survivor of a flock of gobblers that formerly roamed together.

The hermit gobbler knows from long experience the hunters' tactics that have killed his companions, and he has become silent and remote. In his travels, he keeps well away from all logs, stumps, and thickets from which a hunter can shoot him from ambush, and he will not answer the call of another turkey unless it is in the breeding season. He seldom flies, but walks or runs through the woods and keeps trees or bushes between himself and any object that arouses his suspicion.

As I studied the black gobbler, it became more and more apparent—just as Rufus had told me—that he came to Willow Oak Swamp and the Mason Farm not only for food, but for protection. The entire farm, including the eastern part of Willow Oak Swamp, west to the crest of Laurel Hill and south into Siler's

Bog, had been posted by the university officials against trespass. It was the last refuge of the black gobbler over his known range, and he came there, especially during the hunting season, after he had been shot at outside the farm.

Meanwhile I talked with hunters, besides Rufus, who had known the movements of the black gobbler. Willow Oak Swamp and the Mason Farm were the northern limits of his range. He had been seen and hunted south to Edwards Mountain and four miles beyond the mountain in Bush Creek Swamp. I was learning why I might not see him for months at a time on the Mason Farm. Apparently he traveled over a valley and wooded hills two miles wide and at least nine miles long, reaching southward almost to The Big Woods, an almost impenetrable tract of two thousand acres in the wildest part of Chatham County. Few hunters went into The Big Woods because of its bewildering sameness and the great risk of getting lost there.

One September day, when the black gobbler was approaching his ninth hunting season, I visited Cass Carver, an old man who lived at the base of Edwards Mountain. I had been told that he was a keen observer and might be able to tell me something about the habits of the gobbler. Cass was sitting in a chair under a tree in his yard. A hound slept at his feet. He got up, and when I held out my right hand in greeting, he extended his left. I noticed then that his right hand was enormously swollen.

The old man shook his head. "Got arthritis so bad I can't work," he said.

When I told him why I had come, he said that he had hunted

the black gobbler many times in Bush Creek Swamp, but it was so thick there that he had never got off a shot at the big turkey. Each time that Cass had seen him, the bird had slipped away before he had gotten within gun range. The gobbler did not fly, but ran away through the dense plant cover of the swamp.

"I seen him up on the mountain, too," he said, nodding at the wooded hill above us, "but every time it was out of huntin' season and I was without my gun.

"He's a fine ole bird," Cass said. "I used to raise turkeys, and one day he flew in my yard to visit with my hens. He got in a fight with my tame gobbler and just about killed him."

Cass turned and pointed with his cane at the edge of the woods near his garden. "I seen him there about a week ago. He's black all right," he said with a grin, "just about as black as old Cass himself." He chuckled, and I left him to climb Edwards Mountain.

Rufus Blackwater was expert in calling wild turkeys to the leafy blinds he built in woodlands over the black gobbler's range. In North Carolina, hunters are permitted by law to shoot gobblers only. To lure them, Rufus, like many other hunters, while hidden in a blind, used a wooden box-caller with a movable cover that, when rubbed over the top edges of the box, made a sound like the "yelp" of a hen turkey. With it he called many gobblers within gun range. Although the black gobbler had answered the yelp, Rufus said, the turkey had never come within shooting range.

"He'll gobble once," said Rufus, "then I won't hear from him because he's circlin' me to get a better look. Three times I've turned in my blind and seen him peekin' from behind a tree, watchin' and listenin' but with no intention of comin' closer."

One fall day, just before the hunting season, Rufus showed me a blind he had built the year before of logs and the lopped branches of oaks to which the brown leaves still clung. It was beside an old logging road that had been cut years before along the wooded crest of Laurel Hill. Around the outside Rufus had shoved into the ground the cut green branches of pine trees. From inside he could see past the blind and through the leafless fall woods in any direction and yet be screened from the eyesight of the wariest wild turkey.

With his respect for the law, and his knowledge of wild turkey habits, Rufus had selected the place with great care. It was just outside the posted limits of the Mason Farm property line, and the blind overlooked the forest floor to the west, beneath a grove of oak trees. There the last flocks of wild turkeys on the Mason Farm had come up from Willow Oak Swamp in the morning and late afternoon to scratch for acorns that are so abundant beneath the fallen leaves.

Rufus pointed to a sandy rut in the road. "Last summer the gobbler crossed the road at this place at least fifty times on his way from the swamp to the oak grove. If there's any weakness in a wild turkey it's in his fixed habits. I built the blind here thinkin' I could bushwhack the black gobbler some mornin' on his way to his feedin' ground. But he outsmarted me. The minute he discovered the blind, he stopped crossin' at this place and must have come to the grove from another direction. I stopped hidin' here, thinkin' he'd get confident again after he'd found there was no danger. It's been a year now, but I'm bettin' that he's still goin' to pass here someday."

Again I tried to persuade Rufus that the black gobbler deserved to live, but he did not answer and appeared not to hear me. The man seemed more than ever obsessed with killing the old gobbler.

In that autumn of the gobbler's tenth year, I saw him on three successive days, and, in the language of turkey hunters, I "roosted" him each time. One evening in November, I was standing just north of Morgan Creek in the twilight, beside a road at the bottom of a ridge of loblolly pines. I was almost on the northern border of the Mason Farm and had been stopped in my tracks by the sharp bark of a fox. The sound had come from the south, in the direction of Big Oak Woods. I stood listening, my back to one of the pines.

Suddenly, in front of me and barely clearing the tall trees by Morgan Creek, I saw a large bird flying toward me. It began to glide downward, coming almost directly toward my position. Its big wings were opened wide, its long neck extended, its legs held straight back under its partly spread tail. I knew instantly that this bird was the black gobbler. In the fading light he had not seen me standing under the dark pines.

As he came toward me, he suddenly dipped one wing and turned sharply away. Two hundred feet from the place where I stood, he alighted on the road, ran a few steps, then stopped. I had not moved except to turn my head slowly to watch his flight. In the gloom he stood for a moment longer, his head high, his body tense as he looked and listened. Then he sprang into the air and flapped upward to a lower branch of one of the pines by the road. I heard his wings slapping the limbs as he flew from one branch to another, going higher and higher in the tree. Then he was silent, and I knew that he had settled on his roost for the night.

I remembered Rufus's remark about the fixity of habits of wild turkeys. When roosting time comes they are possessed of a single purpose: to fly from the ground to a suitable perch for the night. Usually, between three and four o'clock in the afternoon, a flock will start a leisurely movement toward the roost, but if starting late, they may run to get there on time, and at sunset will often fly long distances to reach the roost before dark. Apparently, on this November day the black gobbler had started late for his home roost. And home it can be, to which a flock, and especially a hermit gobbler, will return day after day—if undisturbed in their sleep—a place where one turkey day ends and the next one begins.

For three days I came each evening to the black gobbler's roosting place and hid by the side of the road. I wanted to be sure that no trespasser was there to greet the home-coming gobbler with a load of shot, and I wanted to see how many days in succession he would return. From the accumulated dung under his night perch in the big pine, I guessed that he had been using the same sleeping place for at least a month.

For three nights the gobbler came to his roost without seeing me in my hiding place. And each evening he used the same approach that I had seen that first day. But on the fourth evening he did not come. That day the hunting season had opened, the tenth for the old gobbler.

When my telephone rang at nine o'clock that night, it was Rufus calling. Before he began to talk, I suspected what he would have to tell me.

"I told you turkeys have fixed habits," he said. "I was in the blind this morning at first daylight. I waited two hours before I heard somethin' comin' through the woods. When a turkey walks in dry leaves he can make as much noise as a man, and I wasn't sure but what it was another hunter."

Rufus paused, but when I did not speak, he went on.

"He walked right past the blind, with no more than a glance at it. I was thinkin' of you and I was goin' to let him go. But when he got a hundred feet away and I thought I was goin' to lose him, I couldn't stop myself. I raised up clear of the blind and shot him just as he stepped behind a tree. It was not a head shot, like I planned, and if I hadn't hesitated I would have killed him outright.

"He flew straight up in the air, goin' higher and higher until he was over the treetops. When he went out of sight, instead of scalin' down on set wings, he was flutterin' them like a turkey that's been hit. I hunted him all day, searchin' in every brush pile and thicket from Laurel Hill to the swamp, but I never found him. I think he's alive, but I got a hunch that nobody's goin' to see him again."

And no one, as far as I know, ever saw the black gobbler after that. For a week I searched for him in Willow Oak Swamp, hoping that if I did find the wounded bird I might save him. I had one hope: if he was still alive, he might have gone southward over his wooded range to The Big Woods. Once there, he would be safe in the almost impassable, little-hunted interior. Other famous gobblers had escaped after being shot—Three Toes and Broken Foot, both of the South Carolina swamps and foothills, and a Florida turkey so smart and elusive that he was called by hunters The Phantom. Although shot and wounded at least once, each of these turkeys was thought to have lived out its life of up to twelve or fourteen years and to have died of natural causes.

At dawn one November morning, almost a year after the black gobbler had been shot, I was walking along the south border of Big Oak Woods by a broad field. From beyond the weeds and grasses deep in Siler's Bog I heard a barred owl call. Then, far away in Willow Oak Swamp, I heard a faint answering call of a wild turkey. I listened, standing silent for a long while, but the sound was not repeated. I had no hope that it might be the black one. With his years of wisdom, he would not have answered any call that would have revealed his position to a hunter. But a young gobbler in his first autumn would.

I heard no more swamp sounds, but closeby I listened to the tinkling chorus of ground crickets that would run on and on until the frost had stilled their voices in the grass. The rising sun sent long shafts of light across the old field. I heard the autumn song of a meadowlark, piercing, sweet, and clear. I started for Willow Oak Swamp in search of the young gobbler.